Mary Wollstonecraft: A Very Short Introduction

VERY SHORT INTRODUCTIONS are for anyone wanting a stimulating and accessible way into a new subject. They are written by experts, and have been translated into more than 45 different languages.

The series began in 1995, and now covers a wide variety of topics in every discipline. The VSI library currently contains over 750 volumes—a Very Short Introduction to everything from Psychology and Philosophy of Science to American History and Relativity—and continues to grow in every subject area.

Very Short Introductions available now:

ABOLITIONISM Richard S. Newman
THE ABRAHAMIC RELIGIONS
    Charles L. Cohen
ACCOUNTING Christopher Nobes
ADDICTION Keith Humphreys
ADOLESCENCE Peter K. Smith
THEODOR W. ADORNO
    Andrew Bowie
ADVERTISING Winston Fletcher
AERIAL WARFARE Frank Ledwidge
AESTHETICS Bence Nanay
AFRICAN AMERICAN HISTORY
    Jonathan Scott Holloway
AFRICAN AMERICAN RELIGION
    Eddie S. Glaude Jr.
AFRICAN HISTORY John Parker and
    Richard Rathbone
AFRICAN POLITICS Ian Taylor
AFRICAN RELIGIONS Jacob K. Olupona
AGEING Nancy A. Pachana
AGNOSTICISM Robin Le Poidevin
AGRICULTURE Paul Brassley and
    Richard Soffe
ALEXANDER THE GREAT
    Hugh Bowden
ALGEBRA Peter M. Higgins
AMERICAN BUSINESS HISTORY
    Walter A. Friedman
AMERICAN CULTURAL HISTORY
    Eric Avila
AMERICAN FOREIGN RELATIONS
    Andrew Preston
AMERICAN HISTORY Paul S. Boyer

AMERICAN IMMIGRATION
    David A. Gerber
AMERICAN INTELLECTUAL
    HISTORY
    Jennifer Ratner-Rosenhagen
THE AMERICAN JUDICIAL SYSTEM
    Charles L. Zelden
AMERICAN LEGAL HISTORY
    G. Edward White
AMERICAN MILITARY HISTORY
    Joseph T. Glatthaar
AMERICAN NAVAL HISTORY
    Craig L. Symonds
AMERICAN POETRY David Caplan
AMERICAN POLITICAL HISTORY
    Donald Critchlow
AMERICAN POLITICAL PARTIES
    AND ELECTIONS L. Sandy Maisel
AMERICAN POLITICS
    Richard M. Valelly
THE AMERICAN PRESIDENCY
    Charles O. Jones
THE AMERICAN REVOLUTION
    Robert J. Allison
AMERICAN SLAVERY
    Heather Andrea Williams
THE AMERICAN SOUTH
    Charles Reagan Wilson
THE AMERICAN WEST Stephen Aron
AMERICAN WOMEN'S HISTORY
    Susan Ware
AMPHIBIANS T. S. Kemp
ANAESTHESIA Aidan O'Donnell

Available soon:

For more information visit our website

www.oup.com/vsi/

E.J. Clery

MARY WOLLSTONECRAFT

A Very Short Introduction

Great Clarendon Street, Oxford, OX2 6DP,
United Kingdom

Oxford University Press is a department of the University of Oxford.
It furthers the University's objective of excellence in research, scholarship,
and education by publishing worldwide. Oxford is a registered trade mark of
Oxford University Press in the UK and in certain other countries

Published in the United States of America by Oxford University Press
198 Madison Avenue, New York, NY 10016, United States of America

British Library Cataloguing in Publication Data
Data available

Library of Congress Control Number: 2024943330

ISBN 9780192862563

Printed and bound by
CPI Group (UK) Ltd, Croydon, CR0 4YY

Links to third party websites are provided by Oxford in good faith and
for information only. Oxford disclaims any responsibility for the materials
contained in any third party website referenced in this work.

The manufacturer's authorised representative in the EU for product safety is Oxford
University Press España S.A. of El Parque Empresarial San Fernando de Henares, Avenida
de Castilla, 2 – 28830 Madrid (www.oup. es/en or product.safety@oup.com). OUP España
S.A. also acts as importer into Spain of products made by the manufacturer.

Contents

List of illustrations

1. Portrait of Mary Wollstonecraft by John Opie *c*.1790–1.

Chapter 1
First of a new genus

'I am then going to be the first of a new genus', Mary declared in a letter to her sister Everina in the autumn of 1787, having agreed to enter the employment of the influential London publisher Joseph Johnson as a translator, reviewer, and author. She wrote, not in a mood of confident boastfulness, but rather with feelings of acute anxiety. She had previously published only a short volume on female education, for which Johnson paid her the modest sum of 10 guineas. Now, at the age of 28, having run the gamut of genteel occupations for impoverished unmarried women—paid companion, seamstress, schoolteacher, governess—she was about to enter a literary marketplace overwhelmingly populated by men. With no formal education, she would attempt to live by her wits.

Everyone with an interest in feminist ideas or the politics of the period of the French Revolution has heard of Mary Wollstonecraft. She is widely hailed as the founder of modern feminism. The work that made her famous, *A Vindication of the Rights of Woman* (1792), has a title known around the world. It is taught at universities in a variety of disciplines: women's studies, gender studies, political science, philosophy, history, and literature. Popular biographies appear every few years, charting her tempestuous life. There are many affordable paperback editions of her major works available, including those in the Oxford World's

Classics series. Yet the range of her achievement as a thinker and writer remains little known, and the outlines of her life have often been obscured by myth-making or slander.

This *Very Short Introduction* takes inspiration from Virginia Woolf's brilliant characterization of Mary Wollstonecraft's career as a life lived on the edge, courageously conducted in defiance of existing prejudices and customs. 'Many millions have died and been forgotten in the hundred and thirty years that have passed since she was buried,' Woolf wrote in 1929,

> and yet as we read her letters and listen to her arguments and consider her experiments ... and realise the high-handed and hot-blooded manner in which she cut her way to the quick of life, one form of immortality is hers undoubtedly: she is alive and active, she argues and experiments, we hear her voice and trace her influence even now among the living.

Woolf's perception echoes a much earlier account by Mary Hays, friend and loyal disciple, in her 'Memoirs of Mary Wollstonecraft' (1800). 'Vigorous minds', Hays writes, 'are with difficulty restrained within the trammels of authority; a spirit of enterprise, a passion for experiment, a liberal curiosity, urges them to quit beaten paths, to explore untried ways, to burst the fetters of prescription and to acquire wisdom by an individual experience.'

A central purpose of the present book is to establish that, in the case of this intrepid writer, who lived as she theorized, the stakes were high and the risks enormous. Any reading of her works will be enhanced by an understanding of the odds stacked against their existence.

Being first

Mary Wollstonecraft was born second. She was the second born of the seven children of her parents Edward and Elizabeth, both from prosperous trading families. Her older brother Edward, known as Ned, took first place in the heart of her mother, and in the family hierarchy when it came to educational opportunities, status, and inheritance.

Mary Wollstonecraft was also born a second-class human on the basis of her sex. In the mid-20th century Simone de Beauvoir dubbed women the 'Second Sex', condemned to exist as the 'Other' of man, defined by men as inferior and subordinate. From earliest childhood Wollstonecraft, in common with other girls, was instructed in her secondary status, and prepared for a future of economic dependence, marriage, and motherhood.

She pushed back, rejecting marriage and seeking financial independence through work. Wollstonecraft was not the first woman in England to earn a living by the pen. That accolade is generally accorded to Aphra Behn, who wrote popular plays and novellas more than 100 years earlier. Although in the course of the 18th century women writers continued to be regarded as singular and odd, they nevertheless published in numbers, and in the 1790s would overtake male authors when it came to novel production. However, Wollstonecraft's position in the publishing house of Joseph Johnson does seem to have been unique and something like that of a permanent staff writer. For his part Johnson, a leading figure in the community of liberal Dissenters, acted not only as a mentor, but as a father figure. She served an informal apprenticeship for three years, studying French and German while she laboured over commissioned translations, churning out reviews of books on a wide range of subjects for Johnson's journal *The Analytical Review*, and developing a specialism in textbooks for girls. Her autobiographical novel *Mary* was published anonymously and attracted little attention. It was not until 1790 that she began to fulfil her ambition to take precedence, when *A Vindication of the Rights of Men*, written in a mere three weeks, became the first of dozens of replies to *Reflections on the Revolution in France*, the politician Edmund

Burke's counter-blast to Utopian dreams of liberty, equality, and fraternity. A second edition of her polemic speedily appeared and she finally stood before the public as named author. The novelty of a female defender of the rights of men, added to the power of her rhetoric, made her a celebrity in radical circles and a byword for delinquency among reactionaries.

Wollstonecraft was not in fact the first to declare the rights of women. In 1777 Johnson had published an anonymous work titled *The Laws Respecting Women: As They Regard Their Natural Rights* (1777), sometimes attributed to Elizabeth Chudleigh, Countess of Bristol, who through her own misadventures gained extensive knowledge of the laws on marriage, bigamy, and divorce. The author designed it to inform women about their legal position, with the underlying message that their 'natural rights' had been eroded in an age of debauchery when men had become 'domestic despots'. After the outbreak of the French Revolution, Wollstonecraft was not alone in making the leap from assertion of the universal rights of men to women's rights. In Paris in September 1791 Olympe de Gouges, a prolific playwright and ardent abolitionist, published a hard-hitting 24-page pamphlet, *Declaration of the Rights of Woman and of the Female Citizen*, four months ahead of *A Vindication of the Rights of Woman*. At the end of 1792 Wollstonecraft daringly travelled to France as the Revolution entered its most radical stage and war in Europe loomed. Yet she was not even the first woman to travel to Paris with the aim of sending eye-witness reports to the readership in Britain. That title goes to her friend Helen Maria Williams, who started writing a series titled *Letters Written in France* in 1790 and established a salon where revolutionary politicians mingled with expatriate sympathizers.

Wollstonecraft's claim to be 'first of a new genus' does not relate to measurable public breakthroughs. Rather, it was an expression of commitment to an experimental mode of living. It was about *feeling* new, forging a path outside existing norms. In the same letter to her sister, Wollstonecraft wrote, 'You know I am not born to tread in the beaten track—the peculiar bent of my nature pushes me on.' She constantly formulated and reviewed first principles of critical understanding and ethics based on her experiences in the world and the interrogation of her own sensitive, rebellious, contradictory nature. Long before she even imagined writing a work of philosophy she differentiated herself from 'the tribe' that draws fixed conclusions from general rules and expects that 'because a thing ought to be...it will come to pass'.

This last statement also derives from Wollstonecraft's correspondence, the chief source of knowledge about her life, for better or for worse. The letters written to her lover Gilbert Imlay, published soon after her death by her grieving widower William Godwin, helped to make her a pariah figure. Modern readers of her complete surviving letters have been alternatively attracted and repelled. What some see as appealing candour and vulnerability, others see as excessive self-absorption and staginess. There are many frustrating gaps, in addition to undated notes and fragments that can only be placed speculatively. Although her best-known work falls into the category of political philosophy, and several others are primarily educational writings, her natural bent was towards experimentation with different modes of what is now called 'life-writing'. She produced two works of fiction featuring heroines named respectively 'Mary' and 'Maria' along with imaginary extrapolation from autobiographical fact; works which might today be described as 'autofiction'. Then there is the captivating hybrid that some now consider her masterpiece, *Letters Written During a Short Residence in Sweden, Norway and Denmark*, a blend of observational travelogue and unbridled confession. Personal experience, emotionally charged, finds its way equally into a dissertation on the education of daughters and a historical account of the first years of the French Revolution.

The quality of experimentation joins Wollstonecraft's life story to the unprecedented political events unfolding in France. As Woolf memorably observed, the Revolution 'was not merely an event that had happened outside her; it was an active agent in her own blood. She had been in revolt all her life—against tyranny, against law, against convention.' Wollstonecraft had struck out on her own, breaking free of the suffocating constraints governing the life choices of women. Her rebellion now became part of a mighty current transforming the world. The two *Vindications* were successes, quickly running to second editions, read, translated, and discussed across Europe and the Atlantic. In London she was lionized, and might yet have settled into the existence of a respectable Bluestocking, with a steady income derived from reviewing, editing, and authorship. But this was not her way. She longed to witness at first hand the great trial of democracy taking place in France.

In December 1792 Wollstonecraft travelled alone to Paris. As she explained to fellow-radical William Roscoe, 'I intend no longer to struggle with a rational desire'; caution was banished by eagerness to observe a new society in the making. No matter that the moment was full of danger. In August there had been bloody insurrection on the streets of the French capital; the *sans-culottes* stormed the Tuileries Palace and the royal family were taken captive. A plan for a group excursion with friends was abandoned. In September the radical faction carried out mass executions of political prisoners. As she prepared for her solo journey across the Channel, royalist refugees were pouring over in the opposite direction. The king now known as Louis Capet was facing trial for treason and if, as seemed likely, he was condemned to be guillotined, Britain would join the war against France. Writing to Roscoe, she grimly joked, 'as I go along, neck or nothing is the word'.

In Paris Wollstonecraft was at first bewildered, 'unable to utter a word and almost stunned by the flying sounds'; her command of the language initially failed her, and she was strongly affected by the sombre dying days of the monarchy. Nevertheless she turned

6

down the offer of a place in a carriage home, and resolved to stay in the hope of influencing education policy in the newborn French Republic.

The sudden overthrow of her contacts in government dashed her original plans. War between Britain and France broke out and the Jacobin regime viewed remaining British expatriates as enemy aliens. Friends provided Wollstonecraft with shelter outside Paris, and she now, at the age of 34, undertook arguably her most risky experiment: an attempt to forge a principled heterosexual relationship of equals without marriage vows. It is important to remove the false distinction between public and private politics in this regard. In England, Wollstonecraft had firmly rejected the idea of marrying, detesting the onus on the bride to pledge obedience, the requirement that the very legal identity of the woman is merged into that of the man, and the inescapability of the contract, for wives especially. In France, reformers brought about radical change in the area of sexual mores and family law, alongside better-known attacks on the monarchy, aristocratic privilege, and established religion. In the liberalized climate of the Revolution, where divorce had become a universal right and the claims of illegitimate children were newly upheld, she was willing to entrust her happiness to Gilbert Imlay, an American businessman and author, part of the circle of expatriates. His confession of a dissipated past was outweighed by the sympathy with feminist ideas he expressed in his latest work, a novel titled *The Emigrants* that he was completing as their affair began. There would be no ceremony, but by registering her as his wife at the American Embassy, Imlay offered her protection.

Their union produced a child, Fanny, born in May 1794, but soon ran into difficulties. As Mary Hays observed in her 'Memoirs of Wollstonecraft', 'the experiment was in a high degree perilous'. Imlay proved to be neglectful and unfaithful. Wollstonecraft, overwhelmed by feelings of grief and loss, could not let go of the dream of bringing into harmony her political beliefs and a fulfilling domestic life. She joined Imlay in London, in the hope of a reconciliation that would provide security for their daughter, but instead faced a loveless future alone, with the prospect of irrevocable damage to her reputation in an increasingly narrow and reactionary Britain.

Mary Hays later recalled words from a letter Wollstonecraft had written to her, regarding the slander and derision aimed at both of them for daring to take a public platform and at the same time live according to their own lights: 'Those who are bold enough to advance before the age they live in, and to throw off, by the force of their minds, the prejudices which the maturing reason of the world will in time disavow, must learn to brave censure.' Wollstonecraft's actions were attuned to a future in which women had self-determination and could seek love without fear of the sexual double standard.

It was impossible not to feel ambivalence about bringing a daughter into a world that denied women freedom. But Wollstonecraft approached motherhood with the same curiosity and sense of exploration that distinguished all her undertakings. She studied her own responses during pregnancy and when breast-feeding ('the sensations before she was born, and when she is sucking, were pleasant'), and rejected the tradition of 'lying-in': childbirth, after all, was not an illness. Her little girl would wear loose and light clothing, and be encouraged to explore and to express herself. Observing Fanny's development and delighting in her affection, Wollstonecraft gradually regained resilience, and returned to authorship as a means to autonomy, rejecting Imlay's offers of financial support.

The final chapter of Wollstonecraft's life saw another new beginning, another trial of the possibility of achieving personal happiness in a society fractured by the inequality of the sexes. It was a match between two innovative intellectuals of contrasting temperaments. William Godwin, three years Wollstonecraft's senior, the author of one of the bibles of radicalism and a best-selling political novel, was austerely rationalist, a man who by his own account 'had never loved till now'. They continued to lead separate lives and kept the relationship secret for several months, marrying only when Wollstonecraft discovered she was pregnant. At this point, her previously unwed state became apparent, and some in her circle shunned her. One former friend, Henry Fuseli, commented acidly that 'the assertrix of female rights has given her hand to the balancier of political justice'. But the relationship was not a matter of philosophical calculation; instead, as we can see from the many letters and notes that passed between the two, it was a genuine novelty, an attempt, as Woolf put it, 'to make human conventions conform more closely to human needs'.

Writing in haste

Mary Wollstonecraft never regarded herself as a canonical figure in the making, writing polished masterpieces to stand the test of time. The two *Vindications* were provoked by fury, *Rights of Men* written in defence of a friend, and *Rights of Woman* as an attack on the limitations of educational reform in France. Tradition did not weigh on her. She saw no need to maintain a consistent authorial character, or fit into any pre-given box. Her identity as a writer is multifaceted, and although the condition of women was a constant preoccupation from the outset, she wrote on a great variety of topics and in a range of modes, some of them newly devised. She is at once philosophical and literary, intensely subjective and sharply rational. The writings still communicate an exploratory vitality, and readers can best approach them with an informed sense of the limitations and opportunities that occasioned them.

The first thing to consider is the constant pressure of poverty and debt. Wollstonecraft's feckless father ran through his own inheritance, and then the money intended for his younger children.

The eldest son and heir had legal protections, and since he did little to aid the others, Mary attempted to support her siblings and promote their ability to earn a living as soon as she was able to earn any money of her own. Through love of her closest friend Frances Blood, she then assumed further financial responsibility for the Blood family, similarly burdened with a worthless patriarch. The two friends set up a school together in 1784. When it faltered Wollstonecraft hastily wrote her first work, *Thoughts on the Education of Daughters* (1787), and then immediately handed over the payment to Mr and Mrs Blood to fund their return to Ireland.

The pattern of dutiful generosity and straitened finances continued throughout Wollstonecraft's life, and to this we owe a large part of her output. Nothing else, perhaps, could have pressed her to find a way to write and publish in spite of obstacles and disruptions. At a time when other British authors in France were destroying their papers in fear of arrest and self-incrimination, Wollstonecraft somehow managed to compose a weighty first volume of a projected multi-volume history of the Revolution, separated from her books in lodgings in Le Havre, racing to complete it before the birth of her first child. 'Tell Mrs Skeys,' she wrote to Everina in Ireland, 'it was written during my pregnancy.'

Needless to say, as a woman writer she was the constant target of well-meaning advice from men who thought they knew better. Yet from the start, she was robust in maintaining authorial and stylistic autonomy. Prefaces were a particular flashpoint. She refused Johnson's request to tone down the accusatory address to parents at the start of *Original Stories* (1788), a work designed to correct educational false starts caused by parents themselves. In the same spirit she bluntly condemned the preface to a work in manuscript by Mary Hays, urging her not to apologize for 'Disadvantages of education &c': an author must believe in the value of her own book, to place it before the public.

When the editor of the *Analytical Review* baulked at the way she introduced private emotions into one review, she replied, 'be it known unto you—I will not do it any other way'. One of the most intrepid aspects of *Rights of Men* and *Rights of Woman* respectively was her critique of the seductive eloquence of Edmund Burke and Jean-Jacques Rousseau, two of the most admired stylists of the day.

When Wollstonecraft came to write her last work, the novel *The Wrongs of Woman*, Godwin reports that she suffered from unusual self-doubt. Nevertheless she dismissed suggestions for improvement from a friend, George Dyson. There is a strong vein of self-identification in her defence of the language of a highly articulate working-class woman, Jemima: Dyson should not confuse 'simplicity' with 'vulgarity'. Jemima is representative of those with 'miscellaneous education, that are educated by chance, and the energy of their own faculties' and that 'commonly display the mixture of refined and common language'. Godwin undertook to improve her grammar with Latin tutoring, but Wollstonecraft insisted that there is 'a certain charm as well as sanctity about these little negligences & rudenesses that would not permit me to remove them'.

At a time when the epistolary arts were highly valued, and many a writer prided themselves on polished productions ready made for posthumous publication, Wollstonecraft's letters are for the most part rapidly penned effusions, mixing urgent business, news, and often tortured reflections on her own idiosyncratic state of mind. Many possess a startling spontaneity; few are properly dated: 'I write as usual in haste'; 'My heart is so oppressed, I cannot write with precision'; 'I do not know whether I write intelligibly, for my head is disturbed.' She writes of being 'on the wing', of poor pens, watery ink, the inability to string words together. The collected correspondence ends with a series of notes passed between Wollstonecraft and Godwin when they were at work a short distance from each other during the day, delivered by a housemaid with little Fanny in tow. Hers especially have the quality of emails or phone text messages, elliptical, intimate, strangely poetic: 'I sent no Amulet to day; but beware of enchantments.—Give Fanny a biscuit—I want you to love each other—'.

'She was in the habit of composing with rapidity,' Godwin wrote in his *Memoirs* as prelude to the observation that her *Vindication of the Rights of Woman* is 'a very unequal performance, and eminently deficient in method and arrangement'. While stressing the 'importance of its doctrines' and 'the eminence of genius it displays', he nevertheless admits that it breaks 'the laws of literary composition'. Wollstonecraft had worried about not doing justice to the subject, due to lack of time. She wrote to William Roscoe that on the next occasion she would not submit to pressure to send sheets to the printer before completing a volume. Yet it seemed that a headlong approach to composition was in fact a necessary part of her intellectual process, and was arguably her chief strength.

An electrifying impulse towards discovery is the hallmark of Wollstonecraft's writings. An early work, *Thoughts on the Education of Daughters*, was soberly designed to meet the demands of the marketplace. However, after addressing a series of topics in the approved systematic faction she includes a chapter titled 'Desultory Thoughts' for all the ideas that cannot be fitted under existing headings. Carried away by her subject, the author interjects, 'I have almost run into a sermon,—and I shall not make an apology for it.' A couple of pages later, and sudden digressions coalesce to form a new principle of effective argument: 'Just opinions and virtuous passions appear by starts.' *Rights of Woman* routinely overspills the boundaries of chapter divisions, suggesting that Wollstonecraft is discovering her argument as she writes it. It spirals around its subject and still has the flavour of a work in progress. Spontaneity, speed, and experimentation were absolute requirements, in order to smash through existing modes of thought.

Genus, genius, and gender

When Wollstonecraft declared she would be 'first of a new genus', the choice of the word 'genus'—meaning type, kind, or race—was as telling as the claim to newness. Like many in the late 18th century, she was gripped by the discoveries coming out of the biological sciences, 'natural history' as it was called then. The Swedish botanist Carl Linnaeus had introduced a taxonomy of plant species that took the educated world by storm and extended into thinking about animals, humans, even nations. Examination of the self, the most easily accessible object of study, was an Enlightenment habit that Wollstonecraft picked up in her girlhood. 'I am a little singular in my thoughts and friendship; I must have the first place or none at all,' she wrote aged 14 to her friend Jane Arden; 'I own your behaviour is more according to the opinion of the world, but I would break such narrow bounds.' The letter arose from a short-lived quarrel, and Jane did not take offence, but rather carefully preserved the early correspondence. She understood the terminology in this case: after all, her father John Arden gave public lectures in 'Natural and Experimental Philosophy', and informal lessons to the two girls. She also recognized, no doubt, that young Mary was a puzzle to herself, and that her peculiar temperament was a matter of torment as much as pride so long as she remained in the narrow bounds allotted to her at birth.

Something changed in her conception of self around 1787, as Wollstonecraft stood on the brink of a new life as a professional author. At this point, her use of the term 'genus' chimed with a new sense of her own 'genius'. She understood 'genius' not strictly according to the modern definition relating to extraordinary or superior abilities, although she now found herself in a sphere in which she could potentially excel. Rather, she was interested in the idea of originality, of individuals born with innate capacities or aptitudes regardless of social status, at odds with their environment. She described her first novel written in 1787 and published the following year as an illustration of the view 'that a genius will educate itself'. At one point in the narrative, 'men of genius' are described as 'a rare genus', drawing attention to the common root. Although it was published anonymously, the title, '*Mary*', made explicit the identification of the heroine with the author for those in the know.

Wollstonecraft chose as motto to her story a line from the novel *Julie, or, The New Heloise* (1761) by Jean-Jacques Rousseau, underlining the point that those who possess genius must seek out the conditions they require, regardless of common opinion ('The exercise of the most sublime virtues raises and nourishes genius'). Rousseau himself was a compelling illustration of genius: a brilliant thinker from humble origins, who rose to the top of the Parisian intellectual elite with dissertations on politics and ethics, before suffering persecution from authorities in France and Switzerland for his liberal ideas on religion. He hymned the moral benefits of a simple life close to nature, and in *Mary*, Wollstonecraft paid tribute to his sensibility, his candour in the autobiographical *Confessions* published in 1782, and especially his radically unorthodox fable of the formation of a truly virtuous and autonomous human being, *Emile: or, On Education* (1762). The encounter with Rousseau's ideas was for her a kind of rebirth. She aimed to surpass him by depicting an alternative genus of heroine outside conventional romance scenarios, whose 'thinking powers' are 'not subjugated to opinion' but unfold from inner resources and through critical processing of experience.

'Gender', with the same Latin root as 'genus' and 'genius', similarly concerns birth as determinant and classifications rooted in nature. This was a topic that Wollstonecraft explored when she came to write *A Vindication of the Rights of Woman* (1792), although she employs the term 'sexual character' in place of 'gender'. As she wrote, a determination formed to demolish centuries of hardened assumptions surrounding sex and gender. She may have started

14

out with the intention of asserting the rights of woman, as Olympe de Gouges had done in Paris. But, driven by anger at the writers, almost exclusively male, who had argued that women were disqualified by birth from possession of rights, she happened upon the construction of gender categories and effectively invented the field of gender studies. She cites at length and rips into texts by moralists, poets, and, above all, her beloved Rousseau.

By the time she came to write her signature work, she was familiar with the way the botanical concept of 'genus' overlapped with restrictive ideas of gender, even in her own circle. Joseph Johnson published a translation of Linnaeus's *System of Vegetables* (1783), and works by the foremost proponent of the Linnaean system in England, James Edward Smith. He also paid the extraordinary sum of 1,000 guineas to publish a scientific treatise in jaunty rhyming couplets, *The Botanic Garden* (1791) by Erasmus Darwin, grandfather of Charles Darwin. The work was both popular and controversial, particularly the second part, 'The Loves of the Plants', which graphically illustrated the central place of sexual reproduction in the Linnaean method of classification. In the system, stamens and pistils are equivalent to the male and female sexual organs, and Darwin personifies flowers in various configurations: monogamous pairings, love rivalries, threesomes, and even discreetly worded equivalents to an orgy. In doing so, he pictures a long series of female stereotypes (male partners are barely sketched, since the perspective is male) from coy virgin to promiscuous coquette, their identities all reduced to their sexual parts.

Darwin's *The Botanic Garden* was the great literary sensation at Johnson's publishing house in 1791, when an expensive new edition appeared illustrated by Henry Fuseli, the renowned artist and writer who was Johnson's closest friend (Figure 2). That this work was a severe provocation to Wollstonecraft at the time she was meditating a second *Vindication* is clear from a pointed remark in *Rights of Woman*. She condemns the 'sensual

2. Frontispiece illustration designed by Henry Fuseli depicting Flora in *The Botanic Garden* (1791) by Erasmus Darwin.

error ... which robs the whole sex of its dignity, and classes the brown and fair with the smiling flowers that only adorn the land. This has ever been the language of men, and the fear of departing from a supposed sexual character has made even women of superior sense adopt the same sentiments.' And here she quotes a poem by Anna Letitia Barbauld, another author she knew from Johnson's circle, 'To a Lady, with some painted flowers', including the line italicized and partly capitalized for emphasis, '*Flowers* SWEET, *and gay, and* DELICATE LIKE YOU'. Wollstonecraft revered Barbauld as a pioneering female intellectual, political activist, poet, and writer on education. We therefore need to capture the impatient, even despairing nature of her revolt, and its loneliness, when even friends and allies propagated the idea of women as a separate and inferior species designed to please men.

Of course, women were right to fear the consequences of an attempt to step outside their 'supposed sexual character'. Vitriol and mockery were likely to be the lot of any defender of a woman's right to equal status. From 1792 onwards, Wollstonecraft lived with the knowledge that every false move would serve as evidence for her detractors of the deviancy of her opinions. Unsurprisingly she chose to leave the country, and enjoy relative anonymity in France before unwillingly returning to England in 1795. Severe bouts of physical and mental illness followed. The standard story, first established in Godwin's *Memoirs*, is that her deep depression and two attempts at suicide were the direct result of rejection by Imlay. The reality was more complex. From early adulthood she was prey to disabling low spirits, panic attacks, and psychosomatic illness. Letters to her sisters Everina and Eliza, and a few other confidantes, show her frustrated and sometimes desperate as she struggled to solve the mystery of this inner weakness. Eventually, with *Rights of Woman*, she turns the critique outwards, and in the unfinished novel *The Wrongs of Woman* exposed the hidden trauma of girls and women endemic to the patriarchal household. Sexism and misogyny are social diseases that blight and kill.

Wollstonecraft aspired to be the 'first of a new genus' of women that could live and grow freely, proof against the scourge of prejudice. Abandoned by her lover and anxious regarding the future of her daughter, born outside wedlock, the dissolution of the dream was also a acute reminder of constraints. She knew the stereotypes so elegantly sketched by Erasmus Darwin and

Henry Fuseli that were lying in wait for her, at the far end of the spectrum of female sex objects: the nymphomaniac, the whore. Yet, after the initial setback, she did not retreat into silence or soften her resistence. On the contrary, her final work was the most audacious of all, not only challenging the sexual mores and laws on marriage, divorce, and child custody in her own time, but anticipating lightning-rod issues of 21st-century feminism: domestic abuse, sexual violence and harassment at work and home, reproductive rights. She died after giving birth to a second daughter, before she could complete this blazing protest against exploitation, legal oppression, and stigma. Godwin edited and published the fictional fragment in an edition of her *Posthumous Works*, accompanied by a biography that discussed her love life in frank and unapologetic terms and, just as outrageously in the eyes of readers at the time, attributed his own atheist convictions to her.

The legacy of Wollstonecraft in the 19th century was bound up in an unholy knot with notions of female sexuality run wild and women's providentially ordained role held in contempt. One immediate response to Godwin's *Memoirs* was a satirical poem with polemical footnotes by the Reverend Richard Polwhele, *The Unsex'd Females* (1798). Strangely enough, Polwhele wrote in praise of Linnaeus's sexual system of plants, while simultaneously warning that knowledge of it could taint women's minds. He pillories Wollstonecraft, who had recommended botany as a way of introducing the topic of reproduction to children in concrete terms, as chief among women writers corrupted by egalitarian doctrines. They are a 'female band despising NATURE's law', freakish hybrids, defeminized by their immodest sexual awareness. From the *Memoirs* he draws the moral, 'burst the ties of religion, and the bands of nature will snap asunder'. With chilling reference to the childbed fever that ended her life, Polwhele concludes, 'she died a death that strongly marked the distinction of the sexes, by pointing out the destiny of women, and the diseases to which they are liable'.

Reflecting on a brief interval of harmony and well-being, bathing and rowing at Tønsberg in Norway during the summer of 1795, Wollstonecraft confesses 'the fear of annihilation': 'it appears to me impossible that I should cease to exist, or that this active, restless spirit, equally alive to joy and sorrow, should only be organised dust—ready to fly abroad the moment the spring snaps, or the spark goes out which kept it together'. It is from this instance of self-examination that Virginia Woolf derived her affirmation that Wollstonecraft remains 'alive and active...even now among the living'. Her ideas survived and by this means she continues to dwell among us, less a foremother than a fellow traveller, a seeker after answers, anticipating questions that arise during every twist, turn, advance, and backlash of the long and difficult struggle for equality between men and women.

Chapter 2
The making of a feminist

Mary Wollstonecraft examined the way damaging notions of the distinction between the sexes are presented as God-given and natural, and internalized to the cost of both women and men. Although her interests were wide ranging, resistance to what we now call patriarchy is at the core of her identity as a thinker and author.

The term 'feminism' only became current in the late 19th century, and therefore the 'making' of Wollstonecraft as a feminist involves a transaction between past and present. On the one hand, there is her orientation towards the future. Her personal exposure to the harsh injustices of life as a woman in 18th-century England led her to a gradual realization that the disadvantages she and other women faced were part of a system that could and must be challenged. Reflection on these experiences allowed her to formulate a set of principles and insights that initiated modern feminist analysis in the West. On the other hand, there is the retrospective *claiming* of Wollstonecraft as a founder of feminist thought, representing versions of her life and ideas as feminism itself shifts and changes through the 20th century and into the 21st century.

First-wave feminists, including suffragists campaigning for the vote, embraced a version of Wollstonecraft that brought to the fore her arguments for women's economic independence, liberalization of marriage laws, and increased legal protections. Most played down features of her unconventional life that second-wave feminists from the 1970s and 1980s regarded as vital to her opposition to male domination. Commentators in this second phase brought to the fore sexual freedom and the rejection of marriage in her biography, while at the same time noting in *Rights of Woman* an attack on conventional femininity so fierce that at times they labelled it 'feminist misogyny'. This version of Wollstonecraft quite often involved a mixture of devotion and condemnation, focusing on paradox, contradiction, and even hypocrisy, as if she were a disappointing mother figure failing to live consistently by her ideals. At times she was categorized as a 'liberal feminist' with political and legal equality as the limited end goal; perhaps a sign of the discomfort of supporters at the predominantly middle-class and mono-racial profile of Western feminism itself.

Third-wave Western feminism from the 1990s turned its attention to intractable economic disadvantage including the gender pay gap, the backlash against reproductive rights, and the mental load of gender discrimination from everyday sexism to domestic violence, harassment in the workplace, and victim blaming. In this context, new aspects of Wollstonecraft's writings became visible. At the turn of the millennium, social media technologies with their dual capacity to amplify misogyny and build solidarity have retrospectively encouraged a sharper focus on the power and impact of expanding print culture in Wollstonecraft's day. Feminism today acknowledges multiple intersecting factors determining the experience of oppression, including race, sexual orientation, and gender identity. The Wollstonecraft of the 21st century is still in the making, but ready access to a greater range of her work, most notably her confessional Scandinavian travelogue and fictional works, has helped to nuance the image beyond the dichotomy of the austere rational philosopher and the melancholy Romantic.

The bitter cup

Feminism would be unnecessary if not for discrimination on the grounds of sexual difference, and the resulting damage, distortion, and psychic pain. Some girls receive a degree of protection and support in families that value them as individuals, and limit their exposure to social injustice at large. Others are taught their inferiority from the earliest age, in families where cruelty and violence define their reality. Mary Wollstonecraft was one of these. She wrote in a letter to a friend, 'from my infancy I have drank of the bitter cup, my fortune has not been chequered, on the contrary one color has prevailed, and given its tincture to my frame of mind'. She alludes here, and elsewhere, to what we would now call psychological trauma. At this point in September 1787, aged 28, she was facing financial uncertainty, broken in spirit and fearful of the difficulties of attempting to earn a livelihood as a writer. She hesitates to confide; 'were I to give you an account of *all* my misfortunes, and vexations, I should write a volume instead of a letter'. Eventually she channelled her childhood trauma into several volumes and, while never escaping troughs of depression and despair, she succeeded in reframing her past, from personal misfortune to feminist critique.

Her study of what she later termed 'the wrongs of woman' began with her family. From the start, she made comparisons with the treatment of her elder brother. While her parents subjected her to constant petty restrictions, they indulged and encouraged him. The account Godwin gives of her early years in his *Memoirs* accords with autobiographical touches in Wollstonecraft's second novel: 'Such is the force of prejudice, that what was called spirit in him, was cruelly suppressed as forwardness in me.' She also observed the 'force of prejudice' in the pitiful fate of her mother, yoked to a domestic tyrant. Elizabeth Dickson came from a family of wine traders, Irish Protestants living in Ballyshannon, in the north of Ireland. Mary's father, Edward John Wollstonecraft, was the grandson of a wealthy silk weaver, from Spitalfields in east London. They could have remained in comfortable gentility in the capital, but the family uprooted when Mary was 4, first to a mansion in Epping Forest and then to other properties around the country where her father tried his hand at farming and steadily reduced the family fortune through incompetence, free spending, and drunkenness.

Domestic abuse was the defining feature of Wollstonecraft's youth. She described to Godwin an environment in which her father's frequent explosions of anger led him to lash out at his wife and children verbally and physically. When he directed his rage at her, she was defiant. When he threatened her mother, she 'would often throw herself between the despot and his victim' in order to receive the blows herself. She recollected nights spent lying in front of her mother's chamber door, fearing her father might 'break out into paroxysms of violence'. Godwin's account is sympathetic but also triumphalist. He recounts these episodes in order to emphasize Wollstonecraft's courage and superiority of mind. Her own account in a candid letter written to a close friend who knew her family well, having just begun to work as a paid companion aged 19, presents a different picture. She writes to Jane Arden, 'It is almost needless to tell you that my father's violent temper and extravagant turn of mind, was the principal cause of my unhappiness and that of the rest of the family.' Although she was seldom his main target, and had a strong constitution, nevertheless she continues to suffer 'a lingering sickness' as a result of his erratic brutality. She describes psychosomatic symptoms, 'a constant pain in my side', crippling headaches, and concludes, 'my health is ruined, my spirits broken'. Although she would display remarkable resilience and a tenacious capacity for happiness, yet she lived alongside trauma her entire life. She repeatedly describes, in letters and fiction, the physiological consequences. Her own attempts to manage this emotional and corporeal legacy helped to form her politics.

The key to the problem appeared to be marriage as defined by the laws of the period. 'The laws respecting women', Wollstonecraft was to remark in *Rights of Woman*, 'make an absurd unit of a man and his wife' reducing the latter 'to a mere cypher' (that is, a zero). Soon after her birth, the jurist Sir William Blackstone pronounced authoritatively that 'the very being or legal existence of the woman is suspended during the marriage'. While Blackstone claimed that the concept of the *feme-covert*, the 'covered woman', in common law was a sign of special protection, it denied the rights of married women to separate property, divorce, and custody of children. It was also an abuser's charter, granting a husband the power to control and discipline his wife with impunity. Women effectively became the property of their husbands, and matrimony was therefore, legally speaking, a form of slavery. In *The Wrongs of Woman* Wollstonecraft would go on to examine not only the practical consequences, but also the mental damage inflicted on women as a result of this legal principle, 'goading the soul almost to madness'.

From an early age, Wollstonecraft resolved against marriage. She had witnessed her mother wither into a fretful invalid, dying at the age of 53, and in her novel *The Wrongs of Woman*, gives the mother of the heroine her final words, 'A little patience, and all will be over!' The word 'patience' became code for the bitter inheritance from her defeated mother. It echoes through letters and published writings, at times when she felt fearful, helpless, or low, when action was blocked, change seemed impossible, and resignation was the only option. It crops up in correspondence at a time, two years after the mother's death, when her recently wed sister Eliza suffered a post-partum mental breakdown and revulsion against her husband.

The crisis in Eliza's marriage changed the lives of all three Wollstonecraft sisters. Eliza, after the birth of her daughter, descended into what appeared to be insanity, raving and incoherent. The husband Meredith Bishop asked Mary to come and nurse her, and at first she viewed him sympathetically. However, when Eliza fell into prolonged depression and indicated ill-usage, Mary felt forced to act. It was normal in such cases for the male head of the wife's family to extend protection, but neither their father, now married to his former housekeeper, nor their elder brother, an attorney, would offer this. The sisters therefore acted alone, forming an escape plan that defied legal prerogative and social custom. In their place of hiding, Mary received news of the reaction. She was condemned as the '*shameful incendiary* in this shocking affair of a woman leaving her bed-fellow'. The episode was another sharp lesson in the subordination of women. They anxiously enquired about Bishop's ability to force Eliza to return by law, and tried to map an alternative future. Did she have any right to financial maintenance from him? The answer seemed to be 'no'. The baby had to remain in the father's custody, and subsequently died. The novel *The Wrongs of Woman* draws on the horror and confusion, the rupturing effect of marital abuse, the sensation of being trapped and hunted, the lack of economic support, the loss of a child, all in strict accordance with the patriarchal laws of the land.

'Few are the modes of earning a subsistence, and those very humiliating,' Wollstonecraft wrote in *Thoughts on the Education of Daughters* (1787), referring to 'unfortunate females' left to struggle in the world. The sisters now faced the need to earn a living, in a society that presented marriage as the sole respectable option for women of the middle and upper classes. Working-class women engaged in hard manual labour, such as clothes washing, at rates well below those paid to men, or entered domestic service, often equally arduous, with extra risks of sexual harassment and assault. The Wollstonecraft sisters joined forces with Fanny Blood, similarly placed as the daughter of a wastrel father, in the brave attempt to secure freedom by establishing a school on the northern outskirts of London, at Newington Green. For a while, on the strength of Mary's determination and head for business, and Fanny's varied talents including drawing skills of a professional standard, the undertaking thrived, and Eliza and Everina gained a valuable apprenticeship in teaching. They were aided by practical and, at times, financial support from well-wishers in the neighbourhood, notably Dr Richard Price, an eminent Dissenting preacher and political philosopher, and Hannah Burgh, widow of the author of *Thoughts on Education* (1747).

A female community was the height of Wollstonecraft's wishes at this time. She would willingly acquiesce to life as an insignificant and impoverished spinster, if she could remain free. Rejecting the enticements of heterosexual romance, she sought out passionate friendships with other young women, first Jane Arden, then Fanny Blood. Although the evidence does not reveal a sexual side to these relationships, she yearned for a platonic monogamy.

With Fanny, settled at Newington Green, Mary briefly came close to achieving her heart's desire. But Fanny was consumptive and her condition had been worsened by years of economic anxiety and drudgery. When a laggard suitor finally offered her the security of marriage and a home among the English merchant community in Lisbon, long a haven for expatriate invalids, Mary reluctantly encouraged her to accept. In late 1785 Mary, having received news that Fanny was pregnant and that her life was at risk, scrambled together funds for a voyage to Portugal and arrived only to witness the death of her dearest friend following childbirth. The baby also died, surely reviving memories of Eliza's ordeal. On returning to London, she found the school in disarray, her sisters at odds, and felt paralysed by loss and despair. The enterprise collapsed, she faced possible imprisonment for debt, and yet felt a strange apathy. Her physical symptoms were so severe she imagined she too would soon die. Her first novel *Mary*, in part a love letter to Fanny, ends with the death-wish of the ailing heroine who has staunchly resisted life with the husband forced on her by her father: 'a gleam of joy would dart across her mind—She thought she was hastening to that world *where there is neither marrying,* nor giving in marriage.'

The condition of womanhood, for someone who rejected marriage as slavery, could appear worse than death. This stalemate was worsened by feelings Mary struggled with and failed to understand. She was a mystery to herself, writing to Fanny's brother on the first anniversary of their loss, 'These disorders are particularly distressing as they seem intirely to arise from the mind.' The conventional medical treatments of the time were of no use; a physician glibly dismissed her case as 'a constant nervous fever'. She was not beyond self-parody: 'I am like a *lilly* drooping—Alas!!!!!!!!', signing off the letter to Everina in March 1787, 'Yours an Old Maid'. By this time, her position had, however, changed radically. She was in a fashionable townhouse in Dublin, having spent the previous winter trying to salvage her health and pay off her debts in the employment of Lord and Lady Kingsborough, as governess to three of their five daughters.

Wollstonecraft had taken this step with the greatest reluctance. She considered governessing yet another of those 'humiliating' occupations, and arrival at the stately house in Mitchelstown, County Cork, felt like entering the Bastille. She was a severe critic of the false position of the upper-class women who surrounded her, distracted by frivolities while treated as livestock, herded towards mercenary marriages. Yet materially, life became easier. She grew fond of her charges, particularly the eldest, Margaret, who hero-worshipped her and in later life became an ardent feminist. She sometimes joined family parties and excursions, and met some stimulating individuals. Best of all she had ready access to an extensive library, and leisure to read. Books were to be her salvation. *Thoughts on the Education of Daughters* was published in January 1787, and pride of authorship intensified her desire to secure self-determination beyond the restricted path allocated to women. 'Nothing, I am sure, calls forth the faculties so much as the being obliged to struggle with the world, and this is not a woman's province in a married state.'

Reading, writing, and liberation

After Wollstonecraft broke with the Kingsboroughs at Bristol Hotwells and took the road to London and the shop of the publisher Joseph Johnson in St Paul's Churchyard, she embarked on four years of intense application that led to the publication of *A Vindication of the Rights of Woman* in early 1792. What reading matter and what role models formed her as a feminist thinker and author at this time?

There was no awareness, in the late 18th century, of a continuous tradition of critical thought on the condition of women by female authors. Wollstonecraft seems, for instance, to have been ignorant of another Mary—Mary Astell (1666–1731)—who nearly a century earlier, in the preface to the second edition of *Some Reflections Upon Marriage* (1706), had asked, 'If all men are born free, how is it that all women are born slaves?' In *A Serious Proposal to the Ladies* (1694), Astell disputed the commonplace notion that women should be ornamental, challenging her readers, 'How can you be content to be in the world like tulips in a garden, to make a fine show, and be good for nothing . . . ?' She had argued radically for female education and equal status for women as rational creatures on conservative religious grounds. Women, like men, have souls capable of improvement. This was a doctrine echoed in the works of other proto-feminist writers and a few male allies like the popular novelist Samuel Richardson, when Astell's stand had been forgotten. The idea reappears forcefully in Wollstonecraft's *Thoughts of the Education of Daughters*: 'as women are here allowed to have souls, the soul ought to be attended to'.

Wollstonecraft's immediate predecessors were a network of women writers known collectively as the Bluestockings. Led by the wealthy Elizabeth Montagu, in their senior years the group reached the status of highly respectable national treasures. Their exceptional intellectual brilliance represented a challenge to assumptions about sexual difference, but they made no explicit assertions regarding equality. A few writers of the younger generation linked to them, such as the poet Anna Letitia Barbauld, playwright Hannah More, and novelist Frances Burney, won acclaim in the 1770s when Wollstonecraft was a bookish teenager. *Evelina* (1778), Burney's best-selling novel, cleverly smuggled satire of male supremacy into the story line through the innocent eyes of the ingénue heroine or the biting wit of the harridan Mrs Selwyn. But Wollstonecraft did not look to Burney or any other novelist for inspiration. Her judgements on female-authored fiction in the reviews she contributed to Johnson's new journal *The Analytical Review* were generally dismissive. Wollstonecraft's own thoroughly unorthodox first novel *Mary*, anonymously published in early 1788, may have won no notice but it allowed her to voice her revolt against the ubiquitous marriage plot.

In 1788 Wollstonecraft assembled an anthology titled *The Female Reader*. This indicates some of the authors she most admired at the time, and includes items from such Bluestocking poets, essayists, and conduct book writers as Elizabeth Carter, Catherine Talbot, and Hester Chapone. Extracts from Anna Letitia Barbauld née Aikin and Sarah Trimmer are particularly prominent; they were fellow-authors at Johnson's publishing house.

The outbreak of the French Revolution the next year made a difference to Wollstonecraft's response to women's writing as it did to every aspect of her thought and feeling. She lost patience with the ingratiating strategies of mainstream female authors. She wanted outright non-compliance and turned to an outlier, a historian and philosopher who had the toughness and the financial means to flout convention and rival men without compromise, and the courage to withstand labelling as a 'masculine' woman.

Wollstonecraft sent a copy of her first political work, *A Vindication of the Rights of Men* (1790), to this author accompanied by the words, 'You are the only female writer who I coincide in opinion with respecting the rank our sex ought to endeavour to attain in the world. I respect Catharine Macaulay Graham because she contends for laurels whilst most of her sex only seek for flowers.' As a young widow, following the death of her first husband, Macaulay won celebrity with an eight-volume *History of England* (1763–83) inflected by republicanism (Figure 3). Remarriage in 1778 to William Graham, a man less than half her age, brought notoriety, yet she continued to venture political opinions in treatises including, in 1790, her own rebuke to Edmund Burke on revolution, and *Letters on Education*, where she argued in passing that women are rendered weak by inadequate instruction.

For a woman to contend for fame in the man's world of publishing and political controversy was no small step. With *Rights of Men*, Wollstonecraft assumed the armour plating of a new writing style: authoritative, combative, judgemental. She tested the waters anonymously, waiting for a favourable response before revealing her name in the second edition around three weeks later. The support and encouragement of her publisher Joseph Johnson made this remarkable move possible. According to Godwin's *Memoirs* in the midst of writing it Wollstonecraft was 'seized with a temporary fit of torpor and indolence, and began to repent of her undertaking'. Johnson spurred her into action by mildly agreeing to shelve the publication. The success of the venture placed her in a higher rank of authorship. She eventually decided to use her platform to assert the rights of woman.

In the second *Vindication*, Wollstonecraft again appeared, stylistically, in the guise of the invulnerable philosopher. She could easily anticipate the avalanche of censure and derision that would greet the suggestion that women had rights as well as duties, that girls should have access to knowledge and the prospect of rewarding work, or that the institution of marriage

3. Portrait of Catharine Macaulay (née Sawbridge) by Robert Edge Pine, 1775.

was in need of reform. Even in the sympathetic and relatively egalitarian environment of Johnson's bookselling business, she had faced instances of harassment and misogyny, and these fed into the format of her new project. The *Rights of Woman* is a multifaceted work that can be read in many ways: as philosophy, as a contribution to the Revolution debate, and as a programme for educational reform. It also consists of carefully targeted heckling of the sexist statements of male authors revered in her own circle.

At the centre of Johnson's world was his closest friend, the Swiss-born artist Henry Fuseli, the genius of the place. At the time Wollstonecraft first encountered him he was 46, 18 years her senior, a gnomish, irascible bachelor. He had a colourful background as a bisexual libertine on the Continent, but had by this time settled down in London as an associate of the Royal Academy of Arts, to forge a career as painter of dramatic scenes from literature, myth, history, and his own feverish imagination. He made his name in 1782 with a masterpiece titled *The Nightmare*, depicting a sleeping beauty, swathed in revealing drapery, with a hideous incubus squatting on her torso. The image instantly achieved iconic status, admired by all those with a taste for the dark reverse side of the dream of Enlightenment. One version—he painted several—hung in the dining room where Johnson entertained authors every week.

Wollstonecraft was naturally drawn to Fuseli, a polymath intimately acquainted with leading European intellectuals, who had written a book on her hero Rousseau, and was planning a gallery of epic paintings illustrating *Paradise Lost* by John Milton, a work she could quote by heart. His strange, fantastical art and stormy temperament also spoke to her own turbulent emotions, for past wounds still sometimes felt very raw. She conversed with him and wrote to him. She may also have seen Fuseli as a challenge. Here was a master spirit with the most cynical view of women, seeing them as innately degraded and bestial, laughing at their pretensions to intellect. *The Nightmare* was a case in point: isn't the lascivious monster the product of the maiden's dormant mind? Fuseli shared Rousseau's fears regarding the effeminacy of modern times, once pronouncing: 'in an age of luxury women have taste, decide and dictate;

for in an age of luxury woman aspires to the functions of man, and man slides into the offices of woman. The epoch of eunuchs was ever the epoch of viragoes.'

This aphorism could have been specifically directed at Wollstonecraft, who, referring to Fuseli's plans for depicting the creation of the first man and woman in *Paradise Lost*, confided to a mutual friend, '*entre nous*, I rather doubt whether he will produce an Eve to please me'. She added, perhaps only half-jokingly, 'Our friend Fuseli ... seems quite at home in hell.' On one occasion Wollstonecraft, sorely provoked, told Fuseli to his face, 'I hate to see that reptile Vanity sliming over the noble qualities of your heart.' Although Joseph Johnson generally behaved with fatherly kindness towards her, and she thrived on the stimulus of the work he provided, a number of undated and redacted notes she sent him refer to acute mental crises and an insulting offer of marriage from an unnamed acquaintance. There was something threatening in the environment of St Paul's Churchyard, where Fuseli set the tone. It seems likely that the portrait in *Wrongs of Woman* of a 'worn-out votary of voluptuousness' possessing 'great talents', who both educates and abuses his housekeeper Jemima, is based on Fuseli. If there was a battle of wills between them, he gained the upper hand immediately after Wollstonecraft's death with the slander that she had been infatuated with him and proposed a *ménage à trois* to include his wife. William Godwin believed it, and dutifully reported the episode in his *Memoir*, in spite of the fact that Fuseli denied him access to Wollstonecraft's letters. When Charles Kegan Paul, a Victorian biographer of Godwin, had the opportunity to inspect them before their destruction he reported that he could find no evidence to support Fuseli's story.

Fuseli's tastes and misogyny played a negatively formative part in the development of Wollstonecraft's feminism. Rousseau and Milton emerge as major antagonists in the pages of *A Vindication of the Rights of Woman*. Rousseau's *Emile*, an educational treatise that helped to inspire Wollstonecraft's *Original Stories*, was now critiqued on the grounds of its double standard. In Book V Sophie, the fictive female counterpart of Emile, is introduced in order to be subjected to an entirely different system of education, designed to reinforce her female 'nature' and prepare her to be passive, weak, and dependent. Women should have no autonomy, Rousseau argues, but they can redress the balance by gaining sexual power over men. Wollstonecraft quotes from the work at great length, in order to unpick this twisted paradox, and establish an alternative vision of friendship, trust, and equity.

Milton is another important point of reference, as Wollstonecraft takes issue with his male-centred origin story. There is an incendiary energy to her reading, as she cites his seductive description of Eve, formed 'For softness . . . and sweet attractive grace', and responds, 'How grossly do they insult us who thus advise us only to render ourselves gentle, attractive brutes!' She interrogates passages from *Paradise Lost* line by line, spotlighting the words that subtly establish sexual inequality as a providential and desirable order of things. The title of chapter 1, 'The Rights and Involved Duties of Mankind Considered', suggests that Wollstonecraft had perhaps set out with the intention of a sedate review of women's qualification for rights, based on their capacity for reason. The topics featured in the austere titles of chapters 10 to 12—'Parental Affection', 'Duty to Parents', 'On National Education'—support such a plan by indicating appropriate areas of female agency. However, when in the second chapter she broached the 'Prevailing Opinion of a Sexual Character' via a host of male authors including, in addition to Rousseau and Milton, the poets Pope and Swift, and conduct book writers like Dr Gregory and Dr Fordyce, her imagination caught fire. She pursued the subject of the negative construction of femininity through seven further chapters with an overwhelming sense of discovery. This focus made *Rights of Woman* a landmark in feminist thought, and an enduring source of inspiration.

However, the remaining five years of Wollstonecraft's life, including a two-year sojourn in France and a tour of Scandinavia, led to more extensive and nuanced insights into the question of equality for women.

Broadened horizons

Mary Wollstonecraft was an avid mental traveller. Yet until 1792 the ways in which she understood the problems facing women were largely shaped by her origins in the English middle class. A brief visit to Portugal at a time of personal crisis and an unhappy year working in Ireland did little to expand her outlook and even reinforced a certain nationalist chauvinism. She benefited from joining the cosmopolitan circle around Joseph Johnson in London, wrote articles on new travel literature for the *Analytical Review*, and applied herself to learning languages in order to carry out translations from French and German. While she expressed support for the abolition of the slave trade, in her work up to and including *Rights of Woman* she gave no sustained attention to the lives of women of other nations and races. Orientalist notions of the harem are deployed in order to critique the condition of women in the West.

There is also a narrowness of vision with regard to class in these earlier works. On the basis of *Rights of Woman*, critics have sometimes painted Wollstonecraft as a lofty bourgeois thinker, with little understanding or sympathy for the lives of working-class women. Her condescending remarks about both lower- and upper-class women led feminist literary critic Susan Gubar to label her a 'feminist misogynist'. In *Thoughts on the Education of Daughters* servants are described as 'in general, ignorant and cunning' and a dangerous influence on their young charges, while in *Mary* women of the elite are complicit in their own degradation and the poor are mere objects of pity and charity. Wollstonecraft was inclined to argue that the middle class were in the most natural state, enhancing their potential for progressive change.

Witnessing events in Paris firsthand was a revelation. Wollstonecraft on arrival in December 1792 was exposed to the extraordinary spectacle of working women not only arguing and protesting for their rights, but also shaping political events and carrying their point. The Section des Gravilliers, where she first resided, was a hotspot in the 'grocery riots', and women led the demands for government action on the cost of living crisis affecting essentials such as bread and soap. In the spring of 1793, as the Jacobins took over the Convention, the 'Maximum' was imposed to control prices. The influence of the *citoyennes* of Paris on Wollstonecraft's thinking can be seen in the anti-capitalism that first appears in her writings of this period: a report written for publication at the time of the riots, her correspondence with her lover Gilbert Imlay, and the emphasis on bread shortages in *An Historical and Moral View... of the French Revolution* (1794). Imlay may have been endeared to her at first by his activities as a blockade runner, smuggling desperately needed commodities, including soap and alum, into wartime France. Her realization that he was profiteering on the side, repeatedly voiced in letters, was a factor in their mutual alienation.

In the autumn of 1794, following the birth of her daughter Fanny and Imlay's departure on business in London, Wollstonecraft moved back to Paris from Le Havre and employed a young maidservant, Marguerite Fournée. The two women would remain together for three years, through many crises and adventures, until Wollstonecraft's death. Marguerite is a named protagonist in *A Short Residence* and although at the outset her timidity is presented as a foil for the intrepid narrator, her companionship informs some of the central preoccupations of the travel book. The narrator is highly sensitized to the condition of domestic servants in general, and women workers in particular. In Sweden, Norway, and Denmark Wollstonecraft evidently made systematic enquiries about domestic service: pay, customs, and the legal code. She makes no excuses for her native country England, 'that boasted land of freedom', where the treatment of servants is 'often extremely tyrannical' and admits that almost everywhere their treatment is 'very unjust'.

While gathering general facts, Wollstonecraft also recorded the fabric of the daily lives of women in domestic service: the poor quality of the bread, the debilitating laundry work outdoors in winter ('their hands, cut by the ice, are cracked and bleeding'), the low pay of a wet-nurse who lost her previous employment due to pregnancy out of wedlock, and the song through which the young woman communicates her feelings across barriers of class and language. When, on returning to London in October 1795, Wollstonecraft in despair at her treatment by Imlay planned to commit suicide by drowning, she wrote a note to him with emblematic instructions: 'Let the maid have all my clothes, without distinction.'

New insights into the lives of the women at the lowest end of the social scale, added to her own experience of heterosexual love, motherhood outside marriage, abandonment, and social disgrace all contributed to change Wollstonecraft's views. From early works like *Thoughts* and *Mary* even up until a letter sent when she was in Le Havre with Imlay, although she may wish to alleviate suffering, she takes a more distant and sometimes unsympathetic approach to the plight of pregnant servants and others cast out due to loss of reputation. *A Short Residence*, written under the cloud of her own disgraced situation, adopts a very different view of such topics, and in the novel left unfinished at her death, she devised an outright challenge to the prejudices she once shared. In France, she had witnessed a liberalization of sexual mores, after the legislature introduced no-fault divorce available equally to women and men, and removal of the stigma of illegitimacy. *The Wrongs of Woman* features a heroine who eventually denounces in court the English laws that 'force women . . . to sign a contract, which renders them dependent on the caprice of a tyrant'. Having broken free of an abusive marriage she claims the right to economic and sexual autonomy, only to be met with the judge's dismissal of 'French principles' and observations doubting her sanity.

Imprisonment in a madhouse is the guiding metaphor for the novel, as well as its opening event. Maria is drugged and placed there, torn from her infant daughter by the estranged husband. She encounters a fellow-prisoner, a man who had formerly come to her aid, and forms a romantic attachment that, the final fragments suggest, may prove delusory. More strikingly, she forges an unlikely friendship with a female guard. The character of Jemima in *Wrongs of Woman* brings to the heart of the narrative questions pushed to the margins of her previous vision of the condition of women. Jemima is the daughter of two servants. Motherless and illegitimate, she was neglected and abused from the earliest age, suffering rape by an employer and resorting to abortion. She vividly but unsentimentally relates her history of exploitation while identifying the social norms that have blighted her life from the outset: the sexual double standard as it intersects with class prejudice and economic disadvantage.

At one point Jemima works as a street prostitute, and the documentary detail of the picture shows Wollstonecraft attempting to inhabit the outlook of the 'fallen woman', as if to compensate for dismissive remarks in *Rights of Woman*. There, she had argued that men should support the women they seduce and maintain illegitimate offspring, while expressing 'disgust' at 'the shameless behaviour of the prostitutes, who infest the streets of this metropolis'. In *Wrongs of Woman* the perspective is reversed, as Jemima describes how the town watchmen, greedy for free favours and 'protection' money, hunt her 'almost to a fever'. She is frank in recounting the moral compromises involved. Here 'cunning' is reconceived sympathetically as a necessary survival skill. For a time she gains some respite and education while serving

as both housekeeper and 'kept mistress' of a learned libertine.
Subsequently Jemima is unable to obtain a character reference,
and so the double standard dictates her next downward step.
She is condemned to 'labour like a machine' at the washtub for
19 hours at a time for a miserable 'eighteen or twenty-pence a day',
and she comments, 'A man with half my industry . . . could have
procured a decent livelihood.' After a crippling injury, employment
at the sinister insane asylum eventually leads to her meeting with
Maria, and they flee together.

Some have said that Wollstonecraft lacked the vision of women
as a class that is the precondition of feminist solidarity. This
would be arguable if *A Vindication of the Rights of Woman*
were her only statement on the question. When this work is
supplemented by the Scandinavian travelogue and by *Wrongs of
Woman*, it becomes clear that she was moving in the direction of
a feminist practice pioneered in the 1960s, of consciousness
raising through sharing diverse yet linked experiences of
oppression. Her perspective is also intergenerational. Maria and
Jemima are drawn to each other initially by the reciprocal trauma
of a mother whose daughter has been stolen from her, and the
daughter bereft of a mother. Wollstonecraft frames Maria's
account of her life as a legacy, both an introduction to feminist
understanding and a patchwork of women's stories, addressed
to the lost daughter. Through this model of motherhood as a basis
for intellectual leadership, converting the matter of adversity
under patriarchy into a tool of analysis, Wollstonecraft stakes her
claim as a foremother of feminism.

Chapter 3
Educator

Wollstonecraft was born with a voracious curiosity about the world, but her own education was hard won. Her parents took little interest in instruction, and as a girl she seems only to have attended school between the ages of 9 and 15, when the family lived in Beverley, Yorkshire. Later in life, she came to see this as an advantage. In her first published work, *Thoughts on the Education of Daughters* (1787), she observed, 'Very frequently, when the education has been neglected, the mind improves itself, if it has leisure for reflection, and experience to reflect on.' In *Rights of Woman* she went so far as to 'affirm, as an indisputable fact, that most of the women, in the circle of my observation, who have acted like rational creatures, or shewn any vigour of intellect, have accidentally been allowed to run wild' (ch. 3). During her youth, with the help of mentors, she was able to pick up enough formal learning to make education her first objective and vocation. She sought to prepare herself and her younger sisters for employment as teachers by intense private application and eventually her authority on the subject became her passport to authorship. Education became foremost of the fundamental rights for which she called.

Female education in Wollstonecraft's day was in dire need of new ideas. In 1800, 60 per cent of women in England remained illiterate (compared to 40 per cent of men). During the period known as the Enlightenment, many in positions of power and authority saw ignorance as a tool of subordination. While women of the propertied classes routinely learned to read and write, they were rarely encouraged to acquire reasoning skills or knowledge. If they did, the earnest advice was to conceal this. A reputation for cleverness was considered repulsive and could damage a young woman's prospects in the marriage market. Girls in the middle ranks sometimes attended a day or boarding school, while the wealthiest received instruction from a governess or specialist tutors at home. Historical and geographical facts learned by rote, supplemented by sufficient mathematics to understand household accounts, were standard parts of the curriculum. A foreign language, generally French, was regarded as a fashionable asset. For the most part, however, the emphasis was on ornamental accomplishments valuable in the marriage market: singing and playing an instrument, drawing and embroidery, dancing and deportment.

The position of the Bluestockings, the network of learned women active in Britain from the 1730s onwards, was unattainable by most of their sex. They benefited from rare access to a classical education, usually tutored by erudite and liberal-minded fathers. Wealth or elevated connections offset their eccentric love of books, and they tended to revel in their exceptional status. One, Hannah More, the daughter of a schoolmaster, became a best-selling playwright while still in her teens. In 1777 she wrote a book of essays for young ladies underlining women's innate intellectual inferiority, paradoxically dedicated to the 'Queen of the Blues', Elizabeth Montagu. After the publication of *Vindication of the Rights of Woman*, More would declare, 'There is something fantastic and absurd in the very title.' More's own volume formed part of a flourishing class of writing known as 'conduct books', designed not to educate but to instil in young women the modesty and decorum appropriate to their secondary and dependent status. Works by moralists such as John Gregory and James Fordyce went through many editions, administered to juvenile females as if to inoculate them against ambition.

The negligence of the Wollstonecraft parents to an extent protected young Mary against conventional notions of genteel femininity. She made the most of random encounters with educators. In Beverley she attended a day school, but also received some tutoring from John Arden, the father of her friend Jane and a lecturer in natural sciences. Who knows but her breadth of outlook may have derived from the study of astronomy to which he introduced her? When the Wollstonecraft family returned to London in 1774, a neighbouring couple in Hoxton, the Reverend Clare and his wife, befriended her and supervised her literary studies. They also introduced her to Frances Blood, who became not only a beloved friend but also a role model. When separated, the superiority of Fanny's letter-writing spurred Mary to improve her skill in composition. Nevertheless, the scheme they eventually devised to support themselves and Mary's younger sisters by opening a school was a daring one, dictated more by desperation than by possession of solid qualifications or, at this stage, professional interest.

Thoughts on the Education of Daughters

Given that female education was little valued, it follows that the status of female educators and their place of work was similarly debased. There was no vocational pathway, no college or university education available to the aspiring schoolmistress. Wollstonecraft was to remark, in *Thoughts on the Education of Daughters*, the bitter fruit of this period, 'A teacher at a school is only a kind of upper servant, who has more work than the menial ones.' We know little about Wollstonecraft's school, which lasted a brief two and a half years. Surviving letters are from the latter part of that time, chiefly concerned with social frictions, money worries, and the resulting physical and mental strains. The school seems, however, to have been successful in attracting students at the start, and gained strong backing from distinguished and influential figures in the community. Even after its closure she continued to give personal tuition to 11 pupils, and received at least two offers of governess posts.

It is clear that the period in Newington Green was pivotal to Wollstonecraft's own education and to her development as a thinker and writer. The neighbourhood was a hub for a group of free-thinkers known as 'Rational Dissenters', heirs to the religious schisms of the English Civil War in the 17th century. Wollstonecraft received warm support from Hannah Burgh, the widow of the schoolmaster and political theorist James Burgh, and from Dr Richard Price, the chief luminary among her neighbours, a cleric who gained international renown for his views on economics and political freedom. Dissenters, or Nonconformists, were Protestants who rejected the tenets of the Anglican Church and consequently suffered from various legal disabilities, including exclusion from civil and military office and the university system. Although Wollstonecraft remained nominally an Anglican, she attended Price's sermons in the local Unitarian Chapel and was strongly influenced by the Dissenters' rejection of the doctrine of original sin, and their dual emphasis on reason and virtue as principles of education, including the education of girls.

The main title of her first published work *Thoughts on the Education of Daughters*, makes allusion to *Thoughts on Education* (1747) by Burgh and to John Locke's foundational work in the genre, *Some Thoughts Concerning Education* (1693). It was written in dire circumstances. Mary was crippled by grief following the death of Frances Blood and bankruptcy threatened as the school enterprise foundered. Another supportive neighbour, the Reverend John Hewlett, put her in contact with the notable Unitarian bookseller Joseph Johnson. Wollstonecraft herself benefited in the short term from this outlet for her ideas and distraction from her sorrows while, in the longer term, she was to forge a relationship with her publisher that would enable her career as a writer and last a lifetime.

Thoughts itself is a work riven by conflicting objectives. The opening suggests that Wollstonecraft conceived it as a rebuke to negligent parents like her own. Locke's treatise on education had broken new ground by insisting on the responsibility of adults to guide and instruct from the earliest age. It is best known for the description of the child as a *'tabula rasa'*, a blank slate. Elsewhere he described children as 'travellers newly arrived in a strange country, of which they know nothing'; those entrusted with their care must not 'entrench upon truth' in any respect. Wollstonecraft in the first chapter of her treatise offers a nightmare vision of the nursery, where infants are fed nonsense and taught deceit and revenge, all too often at the hands of uneducated servants. The class dimension looms large, for Wollstonecraft here describes a mother's main task in life as management of the domestic sphere. Failure to maintain proper hierarchy is the canker in the formation of character among the propertied class. The author introduces the topic of schools only to rail against their blinkered focus on 'exterior accomplishments'. There is no suggestion that they could become a force for good.

Some observations in *Thoughts* jar with Wollstonecraft's later theories. A primary tenet for girls is 'proper submission to superiors; and condescension to inferiors', and she exclaims, 'I must own, I am quite charmed when I see a sweet young creature, shrinking as it were from observation, and listening rather than talking.' The subtitle promises *'Reflections on Female Conduct, in the More Important Duties of Life'*, and it is no wonder that a relatively conventional periodical, *The Lady's Magazine*, published extracts of the work in three consecutive issues. In many ways it conforms to the restrictive genre of the conduct book.

Yet while there is a prevailing mood of religious resignation, duty, and constraint, out of this despondency rise signs of protest and experimentation with a polemical voice. 'To prepare a woman to fulfil the important duties of a wife and mother, are certainly the objects that should be in view during the early period of life,' the author observes, but she is outspoken on the pitfalls of 'the married state' as it currently exists. There is proto-revolutionary language in the statement, 'She who submits, without conviction, to a parent or husband, will as unreasonably tyrannise over her servants; for slavish fear and tyranny go together.' This insight anticipates the recognition in *Vindication of the Rights of Woman* that the domestic is political, and a change in the status of women within the family is the vital basis for the reform and improvement of the public sphere. Elsewhere, there is severe and heartfelt criticism of the barriers women face when attempting to earn a living. Even a highly qualified governess was subject to the whims of fault-finding mothers and insolent children, an outsider everywhere, with no provision for retirement.

Mary, A Fiction

Wollstonecraft at this point had reluctantly resigned herself to work as a governess from necessity, but the post she was offered was not without prestige or privileges. Through her friends at Newington Green and their acquaintances at Eton College, she entered the household of Robert and Caroline King, Lord and Lady Kingsborough of Mitchelstown in Ireland. The pay of 40 guineas a year was considered a handsome wage, and she felt anxiety in advance at her shabby clothes and inadequate command of French (in spite of emergency tuition) and fancy needlework. Once installed, however, she was able to observe the manners and mores of an aristocratic family in their daily interactions, and to hone her critique of fashionable child-rearing. In the eldest of the three children in her charge, Margaret (who would grow to become the rebellious Lady Mount Cashell, and later befriend Wollstonecraft's daughter Mary), she discerned 'a wonderful capacity' that would 'in all probability be lost in a heap of rubbish miss-called accomplishments'.

She began to take a serious interest in teaching practice and educational theory. She wrote to Joseph Johnson to enquire after Anna Letitia Barbauld's 'new plan of education' and order copies of a spelling book published by her friend Hewlett: both were experts on pedagogy in her network. More transformatively, she immersed herself in the writings of Jean-Jacques Rousseau. Although she had cited Rousseau briefly in *Thoughts*, she was now in a position more closely equivalent to that of the tutor in his novelistic educational treatise *Emile: or, On Education* (1762). She had the time and resources to apply his ideas to her own charges, and to better understanding of herself. In March 1787 she writes to Everina from Dublin, 'I am now reading Rousseau's Emile, and love his paradoxes.' Rousseau begins with the typically flamboyant anti-educationalist statement: 'Everything is good as it leaves the hands of the Author of things; everything degenerates in the hands of man.' This proposition gives rise to the paradox of the 'inactive method': 'the greatest, the most important, the most useful rule of all education' is 'not to gain time but to lose it'. His proposal that children possessing innate 'genius' can educate themselves was one that Wollstonecraft took closely to heart.

In all cases, Rousseau argued, until a child is capable of reasoning at around the age of 12, education should be 'purely negative', concerned with protecting the child from the vices and errors of the 'civilized' world, and allowing no harmful prejudices or habits to take root. Even reading should be delayed for as long as possible. Learning should be led by the child's own impulses, and reason stimulated by mistakes and curiosity. Example and practical application are crucial, and a walk in the woods preferable to hours spent in the schoolroom.

Rousseau held mothers in high life accountable for many errors in child-rearing. Out of vanity and indolence, he complained, they ignored their infants, resulting in damaging practices of tight swaddling and delegation of breastfeeding to wet-nurses.

Later, through misguided tenderness, they commonly denied children the right to gain understanding from adversity. There is a misogynist tendency in Rousseau's complaints, but at this stage they chimed with Wollstonecraft's experience and she was inclined to echo them. For the moment, she did not take issue directly with the double standard applied to the development of Emile's counterpart Sophie on the grounds that the female sex are naturally sensual rather than cerebral and 'the whole education of women ought to relate to men'. Like many female intellectuals, she was initially attracted by Rousseau's exalted vision of parenting and pedagogy as an indirect route to social and political agency, opposed to convention.

The most immediate result of Wollstonecraft's reflections on reading Rousseau was not another treatise of her own, but the novel titled *Mary*. This *Bildungsroman* charts the development of a character type almost unknown in the world, 'a woman, who has thinking powers', for, as she observes with a satirical edge in the opening 'Advertisement', 'in a fiction, such a being may be allowed to exist'. In other words, a thinking woman required from the reader a suspension of disbelief. Wollstonecraft promises autobiographical revelation—'the soul of the author is exhibited'—and in naming it after herself she emulated the rash disclosures of Rousseau's *Confessions*. But just as he left the manuscript to be published posthumously (Books I to VI were published in 1782, the rest in 1789), so she took the precaution of publishing anonymously. More broadly, the decision to write fiction was an interesting move given the scorn that she poured on most specimens of the genre, including within the storyline of *Mary* itself (the heroine's mother is addicted to sentimental novels). The experiment suggests that it was only possible to express the divergence of the author's unfolding sense of self from the social norms of her time within a work of fiction.

Unlike the author, the heroine is born to wealth. This permits a focus on the genesis of a rebel soul in conventional surroundings, and removes from the picture the economic pressures bearing on young women of limited means, such as Wollstonecraft and her sisters. It also allows for a critical appraisal of elite culture. The first chapter presents a portrait of the heroine's mother Eliza, modelled more closely on her employer Lady Kingsborough, with her beloved lapdogs and fashionable dissipations, than her own mother, Elizabeth. The father is a bad-tempered drunkard, named Edward like Mr Wollstonecraft, who 'exclaimed against female acquirements', terrorized his wife, and thought only of his son until the latter's death at the time Mary turns 17. She becomes an heiress, an apparent elevation that in fact seals her fate, for she is now regarded as a commodity and hurriedly married off to the son of a neighbour to settle a dispute over a piece of land.

The clash between common opinion and original genius is the substance of the narrative. With inborn talents, Mary acquires a character at odds with her destiny through self-education:

> As she had learned to read, she perused with avidity every book that came into her way. Neglected in every respect, and left to the operations of her own mind, she considered every thing that came under her inspection, and learned to think. (ch. 2)

She develops principles of justice through instinctive empathy. A liking for works 'addressed to the understanding . . . taught her to arrange her thoughts, and argue with herself, even under the influence of the most violent passions' (ch. 5). Her aesthetic sense is trained by observing 'the simple beauties of Nature' (ch. 6). On questions of morality and religion she avoids prejudice by reflecting on 'every object that passed by her' for 'her mind was not like a mirror, which receives every floating image, but does not retain them' (ch. 10). Only an equally singular, outcast spirit can directly teach her anything. It is not until she encounters Henry, a quintessential man of feeling, that the company of another helps to expand her mind: 'he had also studied mankind and knew many of the intricacies of the human heart, having felt the infirmities of his own' (ch. 12).

Original Stories and translations

Wollstonecraft's first, defiantly unconventional work of fiction did not resonate with the reading public, and received no reviews in the periodicals. However, while it was being prepared for the press, in the autumn of 1787, Wollstonecraft began writing a more commercial proposition, *Original Stories from Real Life; with Conversations Calculated to Regulate the Affections, and Form the Mind to Truth and Goodness* (1788). The term 'Original' in the title was an assertive nod to the fact that the work had plenty of competition. Rousseau's *Emile* began the trend for presenting a holistic vision of education in the guise of narrative fiction, with character formation illustrated by everyday incidents and instructive dialogues deriving from them. In the 1780s, Thomas Day's *The History of Sandford and Merton*, aimed at boys between the ages of 5 and 10 and their parents, appeared in instalments and achieved substantial success. An anonymous review of the third part in 1789 from the *Analytical Review*, attributed to Wollstonecraft, extends 'the warmest praise' for Day's 'amusing and instructive lessons' in morality and regulation of the passions. The reviewer compares it favourably with another very popular novel for children, *Adèle et Théodore* by Madame de Genlis published in translation at the same time, which, while containing many useful hints, fails by its excessive emphasis on obedience and 'blind faith' rather than rational understanding. Closer to home, Joseph Johnson had already published innovative educational works by Anna Letitia Barbauld and Sarah Trimmer. Barbauld's *Lessons for Young Children* (1778–9) hinges on little Charles's first efforts to read, and *Hymns in Prose for Children* (1781) instils religious faith through rhapsodic appreciation of nature. Trimmer's *Fabulous Histories* (1786) teaches kindness to animals by recounting the interactions of a family of robins and a human family.

Wollstonecraft was familiar with all these forerunners and followed their lead in many respects. Like most, she brought liberal political values into her fables, weaving in objections to economic inequality and social prejudice along with advocacy of animal welfare and active philanthropy. What then was original about *Original Stories*? And why the insistence that they derived from '*Real Life*'? In many ways, this children's book was an extension of the experimental blending of autobiography and fiction in *Mary*. The governess figure in *Original Stories*, Mrs Mason, is often seen as an alter ego for Wollstonecraft. There is a 'Mary' in this work also, the eldest of the two charges, who has 'a turn for ridicule' (a talent the author herself had revealed in flashes in the early works and would exploit in full when it came to the political *Vindications*). The younger sister, 'Caroline', like her namesake Lady Kingsborough, 'is vain of her person'. The scenario stems from the dynamic of the Mitchelstown period: children casually relegated to servants by wealthy, pleasure-loving parents and in consequence 'shamefully ignorant', ideas warped, prejudices cultivated. The mother dies, and Mrs Mason, a relation rather than a paid governess, arrives to remedy the situation. There is not, then, straightforward identification of characters with real-life counterparts, but rather a new configuration of real-life material to create examples addressing not only the remedial education of children, but the re-education of adults.

The stern preface suggested that parents are themselves in need of reform and should try to model future interactions with their offspring on the exemplary Mrs Mason (Figure 4). Subsequently, there has been some criticism levelled at this proxy parent whose methods, it is argued, are overly rationalist and disciplinarian. Although she is always civil to the children and never resorts to physical punishment, she shows or withholds affection depending on their behaviour. Nevertheless, the premise and methods are non-hierarchical. Starting with the treatment of animals and moving on to attitudes to the poor, the disabled, and the oppressed, Mrs Mason leads the girls, through conversation, story-telling, and first-hand encounters, to exercise reason and sympathy in order to arrive at their own conclusions about their

Frontispiece.

Look what a fine morning it is. — Insects,
Birds, & Animals, are all enjoying existence.

Published by J. Johnson, Sept.ʳ 1ˢᵗ 1791.

4. Frontispiece illustration by William Blake in *Original Stories from Real Life* (1791) by Mary Wollstonecraft.

moral responsibilities towards others. They are encouraged
'to ask questions on all occasions'.

Many of these harrowing examples have a documentary flavour.
'The Story of Crazy Robin' is based on the true case of a farmer
driven mad by debt, poverty, and the deaths of his loved ones that
was taken up by opponents of the status quo, such as the leading
radical Thomas Spence. For the second edition of *Original Stories*
published in 1791, Blake illustrated the episode with a terrifying
image of the stricken father in the very act of going insane,
standing over the corpses of his last two children, his dog
attempting to comfort him. Later, as Mrs Mason's young charges
progress, they visit London and are encouraged to deal directly
with the distressed and dispossessed by administering charity.
There are limits to the lessons learned, at least explicitly. The
children's indignation is channelled into private acts of
benevolence and religious reflection, rather than attention to
systemic inequalities. Wollstonecraft's own political education was
still a work in progress.The following year, in 1789, Joseph
Johnson published a work in another educational genre, the
anthology. *The Female Reader, or, Miscellaneous Pieces in Prose
and Verse; Selected from the Best Writers, and Disposed Under
Proper Heads; for the Improvement of Young Women* was
published under the name of Mr Cresswick, 'Teacher of Elocution'.
Although Cresswick really existed, the volume was in fact the work
of Wollstonecraft. There were hints in remarks by Johnson and
Godwin, but her authorship was only confirmed in the late 1970s.
Typically, the preface is forthright, arguing for the cultivation of
mental accomplishments over physical charms, and the
development of true taste in literature rather than mechanical
memorizing of passages for display.

One of the most notable features of *The Female Reader* is the
insistence that girls should be encouraged to *speak* the pieces
aloud, a recommendation based on the preparation of boys for
public life. Another is the prominence of extracts from the Bible

and contemporary devotional works among the literary and secular selections. Wollstonecraft included not only passages from *Thoughts on the Education of Daughters* and *Original Stories* but also four self-authored prayers, two 'private' and two 'social', attributed to 'O'. Religious faith was vital to her own formation and her broad thinking about education. In the case of the Dissenters, it became a foundation for political liberalism and resistance to state power, and Wollstonecraft shows her allegiance to this tradition through plentiful inclusion of writings by Anna Letitia Barbauld. However, she also includes the orthodox moralist Dr Gregory, whose strictures on daughters would be thoroughly demolished in *Vindication of the Rights of Woman*. There was still a leap to make before the language of submission and unworthiness could be set aside.

Immediately before writing the first of the *Vindications*, Wollstonecraft consolidated her expertise as a specialist in education with English editions of two works of children's literature by continental authors. The first of these was a remarkable achievement and one of her most commercially successful publications. *Elements of Morality* is a free translation of Christian Gotthilf Salzmann's *Moralisches Elementarbuch* (1782–3). It required two years of close study of German to complete the task. As Wollstonecraft explains in the 'Advertisement' signed with her name, her 1790 translation includes amendments, cuts, and additions. Well used by now to the mode of instruction through story-telling, she subtly adjusted the political focus in addition to Anglicizing names and cultural references. Female characters are given more authority, a Native American reverses colonialist assumptions, and there is an insight into dangerous factory conditions. A second edition quickly followed, this time lavishly illustrated by 51 plates adapted from originals by Daniel Chodowiecki, mainly by William Blake. Salzmann himself was delighted, marketing a cheap edition of Wollstonecraft's translation intended for children learning English, and returned the compliment by translating *Rights of Woman* into German.

Also published in 1790 was *Young Grandison*, an abridgement by Wollstonecraft of a storybook for children previously translated from Dutch to English. Like *Elements of Morality*, this work, authored by Margareta Geertruid de Cambon-van der Werken, shows the international nature of new thinking on education. *Young Grandison* derives from Samuel Richardson's immensely successful novel *Sir Charles Grandison* (1753–4), which had presented a model of exemplary masculinity. The story of the next generation of the Grandison family is told through the exchange of letters, as in Richardson's fiction, and for the most part through accounts sent home by a Dutch boy, William, who comes to stay with them in England. The daughter of the house, Emilia, is both assertive and compassionate and may have constituted much of the appeal of the project for Wollstonecraft. In this case, too, the author reciprocated. Cambon brought out a translation of *Original Stories* in Dutch.

Education in *Rights of Woman* and other later writings

There is a seeming gulf between these educational publications and *A Vindication of the Rights of Men*, which appeared at the end of November of the same year. The political thinker apparently springs from nowhere, fully formed. The first *Vindication* was fundamentally a defence of her friend Dr Price, under attack for his hopeful vision of revolution, and therefore stemmed directly from Wollstonecraft's time as a schoolmistress at Newington Green. It was there, under the influence of the Dissenters, that she began to connect flaws in education with wider injustice. Her reading of Rousseau aided the analysis and, subsequently, her work as an educational writer at Johnson's publishing house brought her into contact with some of the leading figures in the movement for radical reform.

She saw in her work as a staff writer an opportunity to gain knowledge, and certainly the reading of hundreds of diverse new publications in the period 1788 to 1792 in order to review them for the *Analytical Review* could be regarded as the equivalent of a miscellaneous university education. The reviews were anonymous, and it is therefore difficult to be certain of her authorship of specific articles, but the constant exercise of judgement undoubtedly increased her confidence as a participant in public debate. While she often dismissed works as 'trash' and particularly bridled against frivolous novels and volumes of verse, some of the works she encountered were formative. An example is Catharine Macaulay's *Letters on Education* (1790), which Wollstonecraft probably read in September or October, immediately prior to the rapid composition of *Vindication of the Rights of Men* in November. In a long review in the November issue of the *Analytical*, she notes the way Macaulay placed education as a practice at the centre of concerns ranging from 'The duty of governments towards producing a general civilization' to metaphysical reflections on the origins of evil. This fusion of politics and morality via the question of education, by a female author celebrated for her historical writings, seems to have summoned Wollstonecraft like a clarion call. Macaulay observed that while many complained of the defects of female education, no one had yet offered 'judicious rules for amendment'. Before long, Wollstonecraft applied herself to supply the lack.

In *Vindication of the Rights of Woman*, Wollstonecraft starts by offering her credentials as an educator: 'I have turned over various books written on the subject of education, and patiently observed the conduct of parents and the management of schools.' She concludes that the major source of the misery, historically and in the world around her, is 'the neglected education of my fellow-creatures ... and that women, in particular, are rendered weak and wretched by a variety of concurring causes'.

Wollstonecraft's intervention was motivated, most immediately and directly, by disappointment over the failure of the new French Constitution to establish free compulsory state education for girls on the same basis as for boys. This flaw in the framing of the new republic carried tyranny over into the foundations of the democratic state. It oppresses, she states in the prefatory remarks to Talleyrand, 'one-half of the human race' by prescription, without justification, cementing their exclusion from full citizenship. If women are not educated, she argues, it will stop progress.

> Contending for the rights of woman, my main argument is built on this simple principle, that if she be not prepared by education to become the companion of man, she will stop the progress of knowledge and virtue; for truth must be common to all ...

A line can be drawn from Wollstonecraft's claim to the precept of the United Nations and related development agencies that educated women are the key factor in social and economic progress and a crucial feature of thriving democracies globally. The ideas put forward in *Rights of Woman*, linking gender equality in education and democracy, continue to resonate today.

The work may appear lacking in structure, yet a clear logic is traceable when the theme of education is recognized as the thread. First, expose and demolish existing constructions that inform the miseducation of women. Second, demonstrate, citing Locke, the vital importance of 'an early association of ideas'. Next, redefine 'modesty', so often held out as the primary virtue of female sex and an excuse for curbing their agency and disabling their reason. True modesty applies to both sexes, and is a synonym for integrity in all aspects of life, not just a guard against the threat of losing a reputation for chastity. This leads to reflections on the need to correct the tendency of education to reinforce hierarchy and tyranny, for instance in parent–child relations. The survey culminates in chapter 12, with a radical plan for a wholly co-educational system of state schools. The final chapter reiterates the point that failure to educate women will prevent progress towards freedom and equality, while granting women the fundamental right to self-improvement will enable it.

In many places in the course of the treatise Wollstonecraft continues the attack, begun in her first work, on what passed for female education in the middle and upper classes: those 'accomplishments' designed to make young women attractive to men. By this method 'strength of body and mind are sacrificed to libertine notions of beauty, to the desire of establishing themselves,—the only way women can rise in the world,—by marriage.' The system makes 'mere animals of them' (Introduction).

In a brilliant series of critical readings Wollstonecraft links this error to a number of influential male writers, from the authors of conduct books to poets. But her chief target is Rousseau, whose ideas had inspired the new proposals for national education in France, and who in *Emile* had stated that the education of women 'should be always relative to the men' for 'to advise, to console us, to render our lives easy and agreeable: these are the duties of women at all times'. The contradictions of this position are starkly exposed in *Rights of Woman*. Rousseau, the apostle of political virtue, speaks of freedom and equality when it comes to relations between men. But when he writes of the relationship between men and women, he is the advocate of mutual tyranny and slavery. Despite the advantages men enjoy, Rousseau advises that women can use their physical attractions to subtly impose their will. This may do well enough for 20 years or so, answers Wollstonecraft, while beauty lasts, but, she famously says, 'I do not wish them to have power over men, but over themselves' (ch. 4).

Instead, girls should be prepared to contribute to the common good directly. The free exercise of reason will allow them to understand their duties and instruct their own children in turn. Despite her own fierce desire for independence through paid work, Wollstonecraft presents marriage and motherhood as the main realm of action. For modern readers, this is the most outdated aspect of the argument. In this respect she accedes to the expectations of her time, but also draws on Rousseau for the ideal of 'republican motherhood' that was adopted wholesale in revolutionary France. There was a radical charge to connecting the private sphere with the fate of the nation. Mothers would train their children to understand the true principles of patriotism and 'the moral and civil interest of mankind'. A serious plan of female education was needed to enable this virtuous circle. Much more tentatively, the *Vindication* envisages the distant dream of the vote, and a role for women outside the family, pursuing higher education to qualify as professionals in law and medicine.

Although *Rights of Woman* is generally classified as a philosophical work, it contains concrete proposals for a national school system run on co-educational lines. In this respect, Wollstonecraft moved away from Rousseau, Locke, and her own initial thinking on the subject. Progressive thinkers advocated tuition at home, separate from social prejudices and damaging customs, but the method was inevitably elitist, beyond the means of all but a wealthy minority. Wollstonecraft now argued for democratic education, inclusive of both sexes and all classes. Pupils at day schools would have the invigorating company of companions their own age without losing the tie with the home environment, where sympathy and affections could be nurtured. Schooling would be entirely egalitarian at elementary level. At the age of 9, the paths of the rich and poor would diverge, the latter mainly receiving vocational training, while 'young people of superior abilities, or fortune' would proceed to study languages, science, history, politics, and literature. With its scholarship provision, this anticipates the system of state education ultimately established in the mid-20th century in most Western countries.

Wollstonecraft was entirely hostile to boarding schools, having observed the conditions of the boys at Eton College during a short stay there before her time in Ireland. She condemned the harshly authoritarian regime, which raised slaves who would ultimately tyrannize in turn as members of the ruling class. Her knowledge of equivalents for girls derived from the experiences of her two sisters. In both cases she argued that the practice of severing family ties was unnatural, and the hothouse environment unhealthy in a variety of ways, including the spread of precocious and sometimes illicit sexual knowledge and practices.

Although Wollstonecraft is today seen predominantly as a philosopher or political thinker, education remained central to her concerns. Following publication of *Rights of Woman*, having called for a 'revolution in female manners' she travelled to Paris to observe the French Revolution in action. Soon after, in February 1793, when war broke out between Britain and France, she turned down the offer of a seat in a carriage home because, as she explained to her friend Ruth Barlow, she was 'writing a plan of education for the Committee appointed to consider that subject'. The plan is lost. What remains is frequent allusion to the importance of education in the formation of a more just and equal society, in the pages of the later works, *An Historical and Moral View of the Origin and Progress of the French Revolution* (1794) and *Letters Written During a Short Residence in Sweden, Norway and Denmark* (1796).

Ever the empiricist, Wollstonecraft, after the birth of her first daughter Fanny in 1794, turns to education in the early years. Her letters, and a fragment of a treatise 'on the Management of Infants' published by Godwin in *Posthumous Works*, testify to her fascinated delight at the unfolding faculties of her child, even as she fearfully anticipates the many obstacles Fanny would face as a consequence of being born female. The novel *The Wrongs of Woman: or, Maria*, also left incomplete at her death though with several sketched endings, at one level functions as a guide to daughters for anticipating and navigating these obstacles. The heroine's inset memoir begins, 'From my narrative, my dear girl, you may gather the instruction, the counsel, which is meant rather to exercise than influence your mind . . .'(ch. 7). The device represents a complete repudiation of the prescriptive conduct book tradition to which Wollstonecraft had initially contributed, both in content and practice.

Chapter 4
Political thinker

The storming of the Bastille prison, the emblem of royal despotism, on 14 July 1789, transfixed the world. For Wollstonecraft and her circle, the actions of the Parisian populace against state authority were an inspiration for wider change. The French Revolution propelled Wollstonecraft into speaking out on politics, and led to her contemporary celebrity. In the first years of the Revolution she joined seasoned supporters of political rebellion such as Richard Price and Thomas Paine to argue for human rights, equality, and social justice.

'Revolution' was a cherished term in the vocabulary of the religious Dissenters, for the 'Glorious Revolution' of 1688 had removed the Catholic despot James II in favour of a Protestant succession and a limited constitutional monarchy bound by law. It brought a degree of tolerance for Nonconformists like themselves. Each year in November the Revolution Society gathered to celebrate its significance. But the work of 1688 was incomplete and, while the early stages of the French Revolution unfolded, the Dissenters were already on high alert. Successive bills to overturn the legal disabilities imposed on them passed through Parliament, in 1787, 1789, and 1790. Each attempt to overturn the Test and Corporation Acts failed. It was in this context that Dr Price delivered a sermon 'On the Love of Our Country' to the Revolution Society in November 1790, declaring that patriotic loyalty had to be earned by government, and that developments in France offered a beacon of hope for British supporters of progressive reform.

As the pace of events in Paris quickened, Wollstonecraft at first seemed out of step. She was principally engaged in writings on education, alongside the translation work and reviewing that promised a steady income. She was, as ever, embroiled in family crises. Yet situated as she was, employed by a publishing business that served as a hub for political radicalism, it became impossible to ignore the spirit of the times. This chapter will review her emerging political ideas, outlining intellectual debts, antagonisms, and her unique contribution to the Revolution Debate.

A Vindication of the Rights of Men

The publication of Edmund Burke's *Reflections on the Revolution in France* on 1 November 1790 provoked widespread shock. This veteran parliamentarian from the liberal wing of the Whig Party had frequently spoken out for reform of the status quo. He had stood alongside the Dissenters in support of the American revolutionaries in the 1780s. Now he turned on them and on their ideals of liberty, reason, and representative government. Most specifically, he denounced Richard Price for the suggestion in his sermon that the people had a right to decide their governors, and that events in France should be taken as a sign of the inevitable progress of Enlightenment. With passionate eloquence, in the form of a letter to a friend in France who had asked his opinion of the Revolution expecting it to be favourable, Burke sounded the alarm against attempts to establish a constitutional monarchy across the Channel. Burke expressed horror at the demand for rights by the delegates of the Third Estate and the Parisian crowd, grief at the assaults on royal sovereignty and aristocratic privilege, and a new-found conviction of the essential rightness of an immutable social hierarchy in a work that would become a cornerstone of conservative ideology.

The Dissenters recognized the attack on Price and the Revolution Society as a covert effort to prevent repeal of the discriminatory Test Acts. Beyond this, Burke was exploding the whole concept of revolution as an organic and rational means to improve the human condition. On reading Burke, Wollstonecraft was motivated for the first time to wield a pen in direct political combat, fired up by personal feelings of friendship and gratitude towards Price. The moment of doubt she experienced when composing *A Vindication of the Rights of Men*, perhaps overwhelmed by the enormity of challenging such a formidable opponent, and her steely resolve to continue, represent a turning point in her writing career. By confronting her fear of failure and breaking through the pain barrier she discovered the extent of her own revolutionary beliefs: 'I reverence the rights of men.—Sacred rights! for which I acquire a more profound respect, the more I look into my own mind.' Since her response at first appeared anonymously, the full implications of this self-discovery by a woman did not initially emerge.

Burke had sneered at the idea of equal rights as an impractical fiction. Wollstonecraft takes her definition of rights, natural and inalienable, from the political philosophy of John Locke, affirming:

> It is necessary emphatically to repeat, that there are rights
> which men inherit at their birth, as rational creatures, who were
> raised above the brute creation by their improvable faculties; and
> that, in receiving these, not from their forefathers but, from God,
> prescription can never undermine natural rights.

By making this definition her own, she transformed her thoughts regarding injustice, and especially the inequity in the lives of the rich and poor that had preoccupied her in early works like *Thoughts on the Education of Daughters*, the fiction *Mary*, and the educational *Original Stories*. In these she presented private charity as the answer. The beneficiaries were relieved materially, the benefactors improved morally and spiritually, and social bonds were strengthened through the exercise of sympathy. Charity, she claimed in *Thoughts*, should be a part of the teaching curriculum as 'a practical lesson in oeconomy superior to all the theories that could be thought of'.

Rights of Men presents a dramatic leap from charity to rights as a frame for understanding social injustice. It exposes private charity as a custom that merely serves to feed the vanity of the rich: 'If the poor are in distress, they will make some *benevolent* exertions to assist them; they will confer obligations, but not do justice.' Why should the poor feel gratitude? she asks. They have a right to life, and men naturally hate to accept 'a right as a favour'. The rich must get used to the idea of '*The rights of men* ... grating sounds that set their teeth on edge'. Those who relieve poverty only in order to 'lay up a treasure in heaven', as well as those forced to grovel for charity, are both 'radically degraded'.

The issue of economic inequality naturally led to the role of the legal system in reinforcing inequality. The radical legislative programme of the National Constituent Assembly in France (1789–90), including abolition of primogeniture, appropriation of church wealth, and the ambition for wholesale economic reform in favour of the labouring poor, galvanized Wollstonecraft's ideas about her home country: 'Security of property! Behold in a few words the definition of English liberty. And to this selfish principle every nobler one is sacrificed.' The British penal code, for the most part, simply criminalized poverty, for 'the demon of property has ever been at hand to encroach on the sacred rights of men, and to fence round with awful pomp laws that war with justice'. Magistrates sentenced the starving rural poor to hang for violation of the game laws. The government pressed working men into the navy and army, leaving their families to perish. Turning back to France, she rebuked Burke for his indifference to the sufferings of the common people while he lavishes sympathy on the king and queen. As Paine would observe in *The Rights of Man*, published two months later in January 1791, Burke 'pities the plumage, but forgets the dying bird'.

Burke presented the existing political order as a precious inheritance, and British liberty as an exclusive property to be handed down intact for time immemorial. Wollstonecraft, opposing him, framed hereditary property and honours as the barrier to progress, a violation of reason. She went further, examining the real-life consequences of the reactionary mindset in the home as well as the nation: it was a licence for paternal tyranny and the 'legal prostitution' of the younger generation, who must serve as mere conduits for dynastic status and riches. The political crisis was lending her a new language with which to discuss domestic inequality.

Wollstonecraft avoided mention of the single most inflammatory phrase in the *Reflections*, Burke's contemptuous reference to the 'swinish multitude'; however, with understated irony she deflated another of what she calls his 'empty rhetorical flourishes', with a bearing on women and politics. When Burke described the female protesters who in October 1789 demanded that the king and his family remove from the Palace of Versailles to Paris to address the troubles of the working poor, he writes of 'the horrid yells, and shrilling screams, and frantic dances, and infamous contumelies, and all the unutterable abominations of the furies of hell, in the abused shape of the vilest of women'. Wollstonecraft ventures to correct him: 'Probably you mean women who gained a livelihood by selling vegetables or fish.' It was a revelation to see the unschooled women of Paris taking the political lead, and the threat to subsistence carrying the Revolution in an ever more egalitarian direction (Figure 5).

None of the review journals guessed that the author of the 1790 *Vindication* was female, but the name 'Mary Wollstonecraft' was printed on the title page of the second edition three weeks later, and in retrospect the clues are plentiful. Wollstonecraft is distinctively alert to the gendered nature of Burke's counter-revolutionary language. 'Manliness' was an integral part of arguments for rights and liberty. This was a legacy of classical

5. A contemporary image of the Women's March to Versailles on 5 October 1789.

republicanism, known as the Commonwealth Tradition in 18th-century Britain. Burke begins by declaring, 'I love a manly, moral, regulated liberty.' A main plank of Wollstonecraft's attack is to claim the manly moral high ground herself, and to cast him instead as an agent of 'effeminacy', the code word for corruption. This discourse rested on the practical exclusion of women from political involvement.

Many critics responding to *Reflections* denounced the way Burke used appeals to the imagination or emotions as a substitute for rational argument, but Wollstonecraft alone dissected examples with reference to Burke's own aesthetic treatise on the sublime and the beautiful, and she did so with special emphasis on the invidious sexism underlying both the aesthetic system and the political rhetoric. She condemned in both the substitution of pleasing appearances for moral substance, even going so far as to hold him accountable for women who cultivate prettiness, but seem to have no souls. She alludes to an example recently reported in the Commons during the debates on abolition of the slave trade: a West Indian planter's wife who orders the flagellation of a slave, then sheds a tear on reading a sentimental novel. His 'servile eulogiums' on the beauty of the French queen and lamentation that 'the age of chivalry is gone' represents a comparable short-circuiting of rational argument and moral principle. She cannot resist digressing to observe that 'such homage' has the effect of making women 'vain inconsiderate dolls'.

Burke claimed unapologetically that his opinions derived from 'natural' emotion and imagination, leading Wollstonecraft and others to insist on the overriding importance of reason. In Wollstonecraft's case, this has caused confusion. How is it that she can praise imagination and sensibility to the skies in works before and after the *Vindications*, yet damn them in her most explicitly political writings. The apparent contradiction can be explained by the pragmatic demands of political polemic. Feelings of anger, compassion, and sympathy are not absent from the *Vindications*. After all, *Rights of Men* was avowedly motivated by sympathy for a friend, Dr Price. Nor are imaginative flights absent. However, it was strategically important to lay claim to rationality, and demonstrate it rhetorically.

The Declaration of the Rights of Man and of the Citizen issued by the French National Constituent Assembly in August 1789 inevitably raised questions about the condition of enslaved Africans in the West Indian colonies, denied every human right. In October 1790, Victor Ogé, a free man of colour, led an insurgency in the French colony of Saint-Domingue on the island of Hispaniola demanding the right to vote. It was suppressed a few months later, the leader broken on the wheel. At the time European abolitionists shrank from applying the language of rights to their cause, fearing it would be counter-productive and preferring to stimulate pity as a tactic. Wollstonecraft several times refers to the misery of the enslaved, in contrast to Burke's compassion for the privileged alone, but she stops short of insisting on their rights.

She also dwells briefly on ways in which women are rendered incapable of exercising reason and therefore unfit for possessing rights. It is possible to identify precisely the seed of the *Rights of Woman* in the *Rights of Men* when she quotes Burke citing Hamlet's misogynist rant at Ophelia in Act III of Shakespeare's play to argue that women's appeal for men depends on cultivating artificial weakness: 'they should, "learn to lisp, to totter in their walk and nickname God's creatures"'. The allusion to Hamlet reappears in the Introduction to the second *Vindication*, again making the point that 'strength of body and mind are sacrificed to libertine notions of beauty' as women try to establish themselves in the world through the only means open to them: marriage.

The reception of *Rights of Men* after her authorship was revealed would have strengthened her resolve to defy the sexual double standard regarding intellect as well as morality. She was ridiculed and patronized, and even those on her own side suddenly found fault with the treatise's impetuous organization and grammar, and 'disrespectful' tone towards a great man. William Godwin met Wollstonecraft for the first time at one of Joseph Johnson's weekly dinner parties a year later, and resented having to listen to her opinions when he would have preferred to hear from another guest, Tom Paine, regarded as Burke's main antagonist. On this point Godwin's attitude resembled that of Burke: to be properly feminine, women should be seen and not heard.

No wonder that Wollstonecraft sought moral support from the only other woman who had openly contested political ideas, the philosopher and historian Catharine Macaulay, sending her the second edition of *Rights of Men*. The warm reply she received must have felt like the passing of the mantle when Macaulay died six months later, in June 1791. The responsibility for vindicating the rights of woman now lay with Wollstonecraft herself.

A Vindication of the Rights of Woman

Wollstonecraft's next foray into the war of ideas was more considered, more original, and even more personal. To William Roscoe, who had commissioned a painting of her, she stated that the new book would be a self-portrait, '*I* myself . . . shall certainly appear, head and heart.' With the encouragement of her publisher, she wrote this second political treatise calling for an extension of the new egalitarianism to include the female sex, and for a 'revolution in manners' deriving from women themselves. She retained the term *Vindication* as her brand, with its suggestion of Amazonian attack, but this time chose to talk of 'Woman' rather than 'women', endowing the claims with philosophical validity. The subtitle is *Strictures on Political and Moral Subjects*, a clear assertion of the right of a woman to present opinions on politics as well as the safer terrain of morality (Figure 6).

On the opening page, *Rights of Woman* addressed a leading member of the French revolutionary government, Talleyrand, who had recently published a report recommending a compulsory state education system freely available to all; apart from girls. In making this exception, legislators were consciously following the path marked out by Rousseau in *Emile*. This was an invitation to Wollstonecraft, with her practical experience in education and prior reflection on female education and Rousseau specifically. As in the case of *Rights of Men*, she felt compelled to respond. The plan was to demolish the case for treating half the population like a separate species, and make proposals to encourage girls to acquire physical strength and intellectual and moral independence. She was directly intervening in French debate on the creation of a democratic political order, urging Talleyrand to reconsider.

Wollstonecraft now recognized that education, the field in which she had toiled for most of her adult life, was the main driver of

A

VINDICATION

OF THE

RIGHTS OF WOMAN:

WITH

STRICTURES

ON

POLITICAL AND MORAL SUBJECTS.

By MARY WOLLSTONECRAFT.

LONDON:

PRINTED FOR J. JOHNSON, N° 72, ST. PAUL'S CHURCH YARD.

1792.

8° ℔. 426. Jun

6. The title page of *A Vindication of the Rights of Woman* (1792).

progress. Locke's theory of the association of ideas, cited in *Rights of Woman*, suggested that a new politics depended on a new egalitarian selfhood shaped by enlightened principles from the cradle. France must not carry the contamination of irrational hierarchy into the new era. Talleyrand himself had admitted in his report 'that to see one half of the human race excluded by the other from all participation of government, was a political phenomenon that, according to abstract principles, it was impossible to explain', yet still he insisted on this residue of the old order, the subordination of women. This was a surrender to custom and prescription, and a betrayal of the revolutionary philosophy of rights.

In her response, Wollstonecraft warned, 'till women are more rationally educated, the progress of human virtue and improvement in knowledge must receive continual checks'. She continued with a rallying cry:

> It is time to effect a revolution in female manners—time to restore to them their lost dignity—and make them, as a part of the human species, labour by reforming themselves to reform the world. (ch. 3)

This, and the title, sound radical. By 'manners' she meant nothing less than fundamental ideas of worth, and to call on women themselves to lead the change was to acknowledge their latent power. Yet interestingly, when the work first appeared it was welcomed by many as a sensible proposal for educational reform. At this moment, the political climate still tilted towards liberalism. Furthermore, a great deal of her programme coincided with that of reformers who based their arguments on religion rather than rights. The conservative Evangelical Hannah More similarly advised a more rational and moral mode of education, and emphasized motherhood and family duties as a means by which women could contribute to social improvement. She also shared the view that the slave trade must be abolished.

Commentators have sometimes pointed out that in *Rights of Woman*, the author seems more concerned to define the duties of women than their rights. It is not clear that Wollstonecraft even envisages votes for women or active participation in government. There is no mention of higher education, and the prospect of women working as equals in such professions as law and medicine is barely touched on. Instead the family provides the essential paradigm. It is not that Wollstonecraft had become a convert to the marriage contract. As in the first *Vindication* she refers to marriage merely for subsistence or a financial settlement as 'legal prostitution'. Nevertheless she attempted to reimagine the institution in a way that would allow women to thrive and realize their capabilities. The relationship between husband and wife would be based on friendship and mutual respect. Women would play their part as citizens primarily by judicious management of the household and by raising future citizens with intelligence and moral integrity.

This cautious vision of duties becomes a plank for the bold claim to rights, the foundation for as yet unimaginable modes of existence. The first duty of women is 'to themselves as rational creatures' (ch. 9). Duty is envisaged not as self-sacrifice, but as a means to develop the faculties and allow autonomy. In the meantime, on one right Wollstonecraft was adamant: the right of girls to education. They must receive the same opportunities as boys to strengthen their bodies and expand their minds. In the course of her argument, alongside the critique of the condition of women, she continued to fire salvos at the targets identified in *Rights of Men*: the monarchy, the army, the plutocracy, comparable strongholds of irrational hierarchy and corruption. Her political position is disruptive, manifested in an exploratory style of writing. Typically, *Rights of Woman* was written fast, within six weeks. Signs of this velocity are present in the wayward quality of the argument, which proceeds rather through a sequence of interconnected revelations, each giving rise to another, than by an orderly exposition of pre-formed conclusions.

The experience of reading *Rights of Woman* is distinctive. It does not present a linear argument, neatly compartmentalized. Instead, the logic emerges in a cyclical way, around a series of key ideas, 'reason' above all, and insistent metaphors, most notably 'slavery'. Themes recur, such as Rousseau's downgrading of female education in *Emile*, reason versus sensuality, and, mysteriously to modern readers, the deforming influence of military life on men. Wollstonecraft returns to these and other concerns again and again, as if trying to work out the connections in her own mind. Any reader lost in the apparently haphazard course of the text would do well to go back to the Introduction, probably written last, to regain their bearings. It is remarkably clear and forthright and contains the kernel of almost everything discussed in the work as a whole. But to capture the path-breaking dynamic of Wollstonecraft's reasoning, it is important to recognize the way the argument proceeds through accretion rather than linear progression.

The table of contents is revealing in this respect. The first chapter title is business-like and responsibly balanced: 'The rights and involved duties of mankind considered'. With rights come duties. The next is less predictable or clear-cut: 'The prevailing opinion of a sexual character discussed'. What is the link between these two topics? Why does the question of rights lead to the question of how men and women are categorized? The answer to this is the crux of Wollstonecraft's argument, as she pursues it through the third chapter, 'The same subject continued', the contents of the previous section having overflowed into the next through the unexpected abundance of the evidence. It is striking that the titles of chapters 4 to 9 all present variations on the same problem that has suddenly revealed its vast implications in the process of writing: the arbitrary and pernicious construction of the 'sexual character'; in other words, femininity as a construct. The method of argumentation is part of the message. It manifests a breakthrough in analysis of the way patriarchal doctrines define reality, harmfully socialize girls and women, and situate them as an inferior class. These mind-forged manacles are a barrier to their acquisition of rights and performance of duties.

Would it be too much to say that Wollstonecraft 'discovered' gender? It is difficult to dispute the indications that she was first to explore systematically the idea that masculinity and femininity are not innate qualities. By addressing education through the lens of the inequality of the sexes, and 'turning over' books on both subjects written by men, she hit upon a realization which is absolutely crucial to feminism from the 20th century to the present. There is a distinction to be made between biological sex and gender. Behaviour historically classified as 'feminine', like vanity or servility, is after all common in certain male professions, such as soldiering or the Church. After identifying the gap between sex and gender, Wollstonecraft could make the case that sexual difference does not entail the inferiority of women.

Reason, an attribute typically gendered male, is the touchstone of the argument. Variations on 'reason' and 'rational' occur 374 times. By adopting it as her watchword, Wollstonecraft was deliberately crossing a line, and commentators at the time duly described *Rights of Woman* as a 'masculine' work. In moral and religious terms, she rests her case on the idea that reason is a God-given quality; it is profanity to prevent women from exercising this touch of the divine. Politically, the emphasis on reason aligns *Vindication* with the mainstream European Enlightenment, fearlessly demystifying and criticizing the present order of things in the name of truth. In this instance, because it is a woman who wields rationality in the name of women's rights, reason is applied to undermine the masculine bias of Enlightenment thinking itself, including that of Rousseau, main progenitor of the French Revolution.

In the course of the work, Wollstonecraft overturns sexist myths that permeated the 'commonsense' ideas of the time, including those of other social critics. She examines the poet John Milton's formative account of the biblical origins of sexual hierarchy in *Paradise Lost*, the routine satirical misogyny of 18th-century wits like Alexander Pope and Jonathan Swift, and Rousseau's paradox that imposing an alluring weakness on women empowers them by giving them indirect influence over men. She also dismantles the advice books of moralists like Dr Gregory and the Reverend James Fordyce, which were a fixture on the shelf of every properly brought up young lady. Fordyce's *Sermons* would make an appearance as an object of ridicule in Jane Austen's *Pride and Prejudice* (1813), a clue that Austen was an admirer of *Rights of Woman*. Wollstonecraft noted with dismay that some women writers embraced the flattering fantasy of women as delicate flowers, defined by their 'short-lived bloom' and denied cultivation of mind.

Cultural analysis, involving the dissection of false logic and delusory rhetoric, was one of the ways in which Wollstonecraft expanded the realm of the political. Another was to deny the separation of the private domestic sphere and the public political sphere. She challenges a 'gender neutral' liberal notion of the political. Patriarchy bridges nation and home, the latter a microcosm of the former. Wollstonecraft addressed critically relations of power and unequal distribution of resources within the family along lines of gender. In the Dedication to Talleyrand she attacked the standard argument that women's housebound existence was for their own good, with reference to the absolutist regime.

> In this style, argue tyrants of every denomination, from the weak king to the weak father of a family; they are all eager to crush reason; yet always assert that they usurp its throne only to be useful. Do you not act a similar part, when you force all women, by denying them civil and political rights, to remain immured in their families groping in the dark?

Women must have self-determination, like male citizens. This revolution that begins at home reciprocally involves political rights.

The term applied most frequently to characterize the condition of women is 'slavery'; variants appear 72 times in the course of *Rights of Woman*. The analogy is explained in chapter 11:

> When, therefore, I call women slaves, I mean in a political and civil sense; for, indirectly they obtain too much power, and are debased by their exertions to obtain illicit sway.

> Let an enlightened nation then try what effect reason would have to bring them back to nature, and their duty; and allowing them to share the advantages of education and government with man, see whether they will become better, as they grow wiser and become free. They cannot be injured by the experiment; for it is not in the power of man to render them more insignificant than they are at present.

The comparison had a long history dating back to the 17th century. In 1735 *The Hardships of the English Laws in Relation to Wives*, an anonymous treatise attributed to Sarah Chapone, detailed at length the resemblances between female subordination and chattel slavery, including the legal ability of fathers and husbands to restrain, imprison, and physically punish daughters and wives. Wollstonecraft's use of the concept is less a description than an interpretation of the political consequences of sexual inequality. Anticipating Hegel's master–slave dialectic, and with explicit reference to Rousseau's theory of women's underhand power, she underlines the debasing effect on both parties. The political philosopher Lena Halldenius has observed the way Wollstonecraft's condemnation of women's slavery converges with the classical republican critique of arbitrary power and assertion of independence as a moral good.

'Slavery', then, was a complex word. When Wollstonecraft was writing the second *Vindication* in the autumn of 1791, she also had in mind topical developments relating to the enslavement of

Africans on West Indian plantations. The preceding April the first bill to abolish the slave trade was presented in the House of Commons. Despite horrific evidence of brutality, the bill was defeated by a large majority. Then in August 1791 rebellion broke out anew in the French slave colony of Saint-Domingue (today Haiti), and reports of extreme violence and massive casualties on both sides soon reached Europe. Wollstonecraft alludes to revolts in the Caribbean and in France in chapter 5 of *Rights of Woman* when she observes, expanding on Rousseau's warning that the liberty of girls should be curtailed or they will abuse it: 'Slaves and mobs have always indulged themselves in the same excesses, when once they broke loose from authority. The bent bow recoils with violence, when the hand is suddenly relaxed that forcibly held it.' While she elsewhere plainly stated her objection to colonial slavery, here she strategically uses the threat of disorder to sway those in control.

The remark illustrates an ambivalence in the point of view of *Rights of Woman*. The author constantly shifts between the perspective of the oppressed, identifying with the women she champions, and that of the male legislator. One of her aims is to persuade men that it is in their own interests to liberate women by educating them equally and granting them rights, as a public good. Abolitionists in France used similar rights-based arguments, and in March 1792 the National Assembly voted to end slavery in its colonial dominions. At the same time, by contrast, the British campaign against the slave trade, based on humanitarian and religious sentiment, stalled in the face of a counter-revolutionary backlash.

The prominent terms 'virtue' and 'virtuous' (321 occurrences) require some historical context. In the 1790s this vocabulary, which had long been a feature of political debate, had a renewed currency as a result of its adoption by the revolutionaries in France. It conveyed dedication to the public good as opposed to narrow and corrupt self-interest. That Wollstonecraft claimed this elevated quality for women was radical in itself; she recommends the study of politics for girls to implant it. Even more audacious is the way, in two successive chapters, she detached the word from the sex-specific 'virtues' of modesty and chastity. This may in fact represent the most momentous demand of *Rights of Woman*. The female sex should not be restricted by a specialized notion of what it is to be virtuous, essentially marking them as property. Not only does this revised application of 'virtue' insist that they are entitled to be participants in the political realm, but it also opens the way for them to become moral agents in their own right, making their own judgements, regardless of commonplace propriety, about what was or was not acceptable when it came to their own bodies and desires. Despite the emphasis on reason, what Wollstonecraft calls a 'wild wish' informs the second *Vindication*: to live authentically (ch. 4). The implications were so unthinkable in 1792 that it was only after the author's death, when Godwin's *Memoirs* made clear just how far she had taken that principle in her own life, that a right-wing frenzy of slut-shaming ensued.

An Historical and Moral View... of the French Revolution

It was no accident that Wollstonecraft's long-cherished desire to visit revolutionary France became fixed at a major political turning point. The invasion of the Tuileries Palace in August 1792 was quickly followed by the massacre of political prisoners accused of conspiring against the government. These events, driven by Parisian militancy, represented a complete breakdown in law and order. The royal family, stripped of their status, were accused of plotting against the Revolution and imprisoned. The Republic was declared on 21 September. Now was the moment to witness a degree of reinvention unforeseen in 1789.

She arrived in December, just as the trial of the former king began. The hushed mood of the capital was almost overwhelming.

He was found guilty of treason and, after furious debate in the National Convention that tore apart former alliances among radical deputies, he went to the guillotine on 22 January. With the fall of the blade, France severed ties with past political and social organization. It was Ground Zero or, as the new Republican calendar proclaimed, 'Year I'. Wollstonecraft began work on *An Historical and Moral View of the Origin and Progress of the French Revolution* (1794). It was to be an analysis of the first months of the insurgency in 1789, informed by the view from Year I.

At the start of *View*, the author looks back to the previous clean slate: the American Revolution. 'The eyes of all Europe were watchfully fixed on the practical success of this experiment in political science,' she writes. America, it had seemed, was uniquely qualified to 'lay the first stones of her government', to design a constitution not 'formed by chance, and continually patched up', but planned by 'reason, at liberty to profit by experience' (I.i). Her main objective now was to consider how revolution took root in the body politic of one of the oldest and seemingly most invulnerable monarchies in Europe. Reason, here as in the *Vindications*, was her tool. The term 'political science' recurs frequently in this work. It was a coinage recently popularized by Thomas Jefferson, contributor to the French Constitution of 1791, aimed at settling a constitutional monarchy, and by the Marquis de Condorcet and Thomas Paine, members of the Girondin Constitutional Project who set to work in February 1793 to produce a new Republican version. When war broke out on 1 February Wollstonecraft, now an enemy alien, disregarded personal risk and chose to stay and see out the consequences of the latest stage in the experiment.

Although initially she often met with Paine, her old acquaintance, and his Anglophile Girondin circle, it is important not to assume her ideological kinship with the Girondin faction, sometimes simplistically described as 'moderate' republicans. This group, led by Brissot, had favoured an aggressive war policy that worsened economic hardship and popular unrest and intensified the atmosphere of panic and paranoia. Robespierre, leader of the 'Mountain' or Jacobin faction who forged a close alliance with the Parisian militants through 1792 and the first half of 1793, was an unwavering supporter of the principle of equality. Wollstonecraft arrived on the scene independent and open-minded. If we examine her writings from the period in France without preconceptions, there are signs that her political sympathies lay further to the left than is generally supposed.

In the sole surviving public letter of a projected series on the Revolution, composed in February 1793 when Girondin free trade policy was in the ascendant but only published after her death, she observes critically that 'the aristocracy of birth is levelled to the ground, only to make room for that of riches'. This is anti-commerce rhetoric closer to the denunciation of food speculators by the *sans-culottes* in the Gravilliers section where she initially lodged and by Jacques Roux, self-styled spokesman of the *Enragés*, than to classical republican repudiation of luxury. Turning to *View*, the opening chapter contains an uncompromising statement:

> Nature having made men unequal, by giving stronger bodily and mental powers to one than to another, the end of government ought to be, to destroy this inequality by protecting the weak. Instead of which, it has always leaned to the opposite side ...

Here Wollstonecraft sweeps aside the idea of a natural hierarchy with a verbal violence ('destroy this inequality') that coincides with Jacobin rhetoric. Given her long-standing concerns regarding economic injustice, she could not be indifferent to the introduction of a command economy by the Jacobin government, redistributing wealth and framing subsistence as a right. It seems to inform the attention she gives in *View* to the grain trade and food riots in 1789, unmatched by other British commentators. Gilbert Imlay, her American lover, began operations as a blockade runner supplying vital commodities in conjunction with the *Commission des Subsistances* established in autumn 1793 by Robespierre's Committee of Public Safety to combat food rackets. When she later wrote to reproach Imlay for profiteering, the animus had a political edge.

On the other hand, in *View* Wollstonecraft does not hesitate to apply a word from the counter-revolutionary lexicon, 'anarchy'. This alone might have condemned her, had her papers fallen into government hands in the fevered atmosphere of the Terror in Year II. When writing the first *Vindication* in 1790, she could pass off the brutal actions of the crowd in 1789 as minor collateral damage, set against the gigantic tyranny of the old regime. Before leaving for Paris, in a letter to Roscoe, she criticized 'the shallow herd who throw an odium on immutable principles', because the instruments of Revolution were 'too sharp'. After her arrival judicial murder had become normalized, and friends such as Paine and Helen Maria Williams only narrowly escaped. Slipping on the bloody paving stones surrounding the guillotine in Place de la Révolution one day, she railed against the new regime. As she completed *View* in the spring of 1794 the rate of political executions soared, and the work reflects the pressing need to address the human toll of revolutionary change.

The reinterpretation of the March to Versailles led by the women of Paris is an interesting case in point. In *Rights of Men* she had mocked Burke's demonizing of public protest and sensationalized account of the violation of the queen's bedchamber. Now she was willing to admit that it was 'in reality from this epocha...that the commencement of the reign of anarchy may be fairly dated', but only because it was a demonstration of the political immaturity of the French nation. She adopted the popular conspiracy theory that the women were manipulated by agents of Philippe d'Orléans, ambitious to supplant his cousin Louis XVI in the guise of a constitutional monarch. This suspicion gave Wollstonecraft a licence to condemn the popular violence without condemning the Revolution itself. Superficially, her emotive account of the invasion of the queen's apartment 'by a gang of banditti the most desperate' echoes that of Burke. But it is crucial to note that she continued to regard Marie Antoinette only as a 'woman' entitled to a normal degree of respect, not an untouchable icon (V.ii). Elsewhere in the narrative she represents the characters of the king and queen with unstinting hostility, aside from a modicum of sympathy for the latter's entrapment in marriage to a 'very disgusting' spouse (II.ii).

The theory of revolutionary violence in essence remains unchanged from the two *Vindications*, but in *View* it is amplified and expanded upon. She is writing *philosophical* history, placing events in the long view of the progress of civilization, using a version of the stadial categories elaborated by social scientists of the Scottish Enlightenment like Adam Smith and William Robertson. The potential for virtue is innate in savage society, but it has been fatally warped by feudalism, its obscene hierarchies persisting in France up to the present. The slow violence of the old regime is to blame for the eruptions of vengeance in the new. Still Wollstonecraft complicates the picture in her overview of 1789, laying some responsibility at the door of the political leadership of the Revolution. She sees with hindsight the mistakes made during the first critical months, lost opportunities to put change on a gradual footing and allow the body politic to evolve peacefully. Nevertheless, she does not renounce revolution, nor the doctrine of human perfectibility that inspired the Declaration of the Rights of Man: 'the people are essentially good'; 'things must have time to find their level' (I.iv).

An Historical and Moral View ... of the French Revolution was well received by the liberal press in England, relieved to find a balanced and ultimately optimistic account in a climate of recoil. One conservative reviewer predictably berated her for writing errors and confused method, and accused her of plagiarizing the *New Annual Register* when chronicling the chain of events.

This last observation throws light on her priorities. She stated at the outset that the historian's lesser role was to 'fill up the sketch'; it seems likely that in her haste, racing to finish before the birth of her first child, her books inaccessible towards the end, she relied on borrowed material for the narrative part, and failed at times to rework it sufficiently. Far more important, in her opinion, was to 'trace the hidden springs and secret mechanism, which have put in motion a revolution, the most important that has ever been recorded in the annals of man' (I.iv). This component was original.

All the reviewers commented on the novelty of her richly 'figurative style' which made analogy to biological science to emphasize the organic nature of political developments. The work ends with the remark, 'the excrementitious humours exuding from the contaminated body will excite a general dislike for the nation; and it is only the philosophical eye, which looks into the nature and weighs the consequences of human actions, that will be able to discern the cause, which has produced so many dreadful effects' (V.iv). Another experiment was the inclusion of flights of imagination, not sectarian as in Burke's *Reflections*, but rather in order to extend the emotional range of historical writing, most notably in a scene of pilgrimage to the haunted precincts of the Palace of Versailles (II.ii). In subsequent major projects, the Scandinavian travelogue and the incomplete novel *Wrongs of Woman*, she would continue to experiment with the autobiographical voice and the place of imagination in the representation of political ideas.

Chapter 5
Romantic

There has been a tendency to divide Wollstonecraft's career into two parts, before and after her experience of love and motherhood in Paris in the mid-1790s: before, she is the stern moralizing Enlightenment philosopher; after, the sensual woman of feeling, a Romantic. The reality is more complex. There are strong currents of subjective expression in her early writings and throughout her correspondence; a Romantic spirit courses even through *A Vindication of the Rights of Woman*, where reason is elevated as the prime mover of progress, and sensibility repudiated as women's ball and chain. Most of the hallmarks of the Romantic Movement—spontaneity, rule-breaking, authenticity, intense emotion, a taste for the sublime, nature worship, political liberalism—are present in her oeuvre, bar nostalgia for the past. As literary scholar Barbara Taylor has shown, the imagination has a fundamental place in her future-directed feminism.

Although 'Romantic' as an aesthetic or historical label gained currency only in the 19th century, after Wollstonecraft's death, she used the term frequently, and often applied it to herself. In the standard usage of her time, 'romantic' often negatively signified eccentricity or excess. It was loosely associated with the heightened sentiments and improbable events of romance narratives. In Wollstonecraft's letters, anticipating Romanticism, the term 'romantic' is shorthand for the visionary inspiration or enthusiastic bursts of sympathy that put her at odds with prescribed forms and 'polite' decorum. It is at once self-deprecating, forestalling ridicule, and a proud declaration of moral independence, idealistically free of the herd mentality. 'Romance' can also signal a certain sense of wonder at her own mysterious misfit nature, leading ultimately to questions about God's plan. Wollstonecraft wrote despairingly to Imlay, 'The tremendous power who formed this heart, must have foreseen that, in a world in which self-interest, in various shapes, is the principal mobile, I had little chance of escaping misery.' If the speculation is self-aggrandizing, as Romantic representations of self often are, nevertheless using the heart as an alternative criterion was an important basis for outwardly directed social critique.

In the *Vindications*, by contrast, Wollstonecraft deployed 'romantic', like the related terms 'imagination' or 'sensibility', as ammunition against ideological opponents. In *Rights of Men* Wollstonecraft placed Edmund Burke among the 'cold romantic characters' of the day, whose rhetoric chimes with the 'false, or rather artificial, feelings' and 'romantic spirit' of 'modern poetry'. In *Rights of Woman*, Rousseau is in the line of fire. It was his excessive sensibility and 'inflamed' imaginative susceptibility to the charms of women, partnered with a self-denying 'romantic kind of delicacy', that perverted his reason and led him to preach coquetry to women as the essential survival skill (ch. 5.1). These negative definitions result from strategies specific to the *Vindications*. When Burke or Rousseau claims the realm of feeling or imagination, she, of necessity, tactically adopts the high ground of rational cognition. However the modifying adjectives 'cold', 'frigid', 'artificial', and 'inflamed' are important; they allow her to affirm *true* feeling.

It is authenticity and salutary warmth that Wollstonecraft values, and these are identified as the features of 'romantic passion' even in the *Vindications*. In chapter 2 of *Rights of Woman* she is prepared to make some allowance for Rousseau's romanticism

as a 'concomitant of genius' and asks, 'Who can clip its wing?'
Later in that work she admits that her own speculative flights of
fancy invite the word: 'My imagination darts forward … in spite
of the sneering of cold hearts, who are at liberty to utter, with
frigid self-importance, the damning epithet—romantic' (ch. 12).

Poetry plays a surprisingly prominent and complicated role in her
political arguments. *Rights of Men* contains a mini-dissertation on
the value of poetic language that derives from genuine passion.
The author declares that 'reason has no right to rein-in
imagination' of this kind (as distinct from Burke's artificial
simulations of heart-felt eloquence). When in *Rights of Woman*
she turns to examine Locke's theory of the foundational association
of ideas in infancy, she begins by reflecting on the nature of 'genius'
that seems to bypass the pedestrian business of building the
understanding through sensory experience. Rare individuals who
can 'see or feel poetically' are able to combine thoughts in
innovative ways and communicate to others unexpected
associations that 'surprise, delight, and instruct' (ch. 6).

It is not surprising, given this conviction that imaginative
literature aids the production of new ideas, that the voice
Wollstonecraft developed as a writer involved frequent literary
allusion, and above all quotation from the poetry of Shakespeare
and Milton. In Romantic-era culture these two writers were
celebrated as the zenith of creative genius and imaginative power.
As scholar Susan Wolfson has observed, in the anthology *The
Female Reader* (1789), Wollstonecraft included generous samples
from Shakespeare and other poets, as encouragement for a girl to
become an 'active imaginer'. The frequency with which she cited
Hamlet, especially in spontaneous private communications,
suggests she knew the text by heart. The hero provided an
androgynous language articulating an isolated, vulnerable,
troubled interiority. In *Rights of Woman*, while Wollstonecraft
objects to Milton's Adam and Eve, she adopts as her own the words
of the rebel Satan.

Wollstonecraft tried her hand at poetry as a young girl. A sample survives in one her letters to her childhood friend Jane Arden. But she seems to have accepted that verse was not her forte. Instead she introduced quotations from her favourite poets, male for the most part, to conjure the sublime. The latter practice was not uncommon at the time, and did not rule out the claim to original genius. After all, genius was as much about responding to greatness and ordering existing material in unexpected ways as it was about self-expression. Wollstonecraft would maintain this practice in every work she wrote, whether political, historical, educational, autobiographical, or fictional. To cite exalted flights of fancy was to create, on the page, a fellowship of genius, and to do so as a woman writer was in itself a transgressive gesture. Very often she or her female creations voice the words of male tragic heroes, ignoring gender boundaries.

The theory behind the practice is indicated in some of the aphorisms that were published posthumously by Godwin under the title 'Hints, chiefly designed to have been incorporated in the second part of the Vindication of the Rights of Woman': 'It is the individual manner of seeing and feeling, pourtrayed by a strong imagination in bold images that have struck the senses, which creates all the charms of poetry'; 'A great reader is always quoting the description of another's emotions'; 'The passions speak more eloquently, when they are not shackled by reason.'

It is likely that the long delay in recognizing Wollstonecraft as a philosopher—until 200 years after the publication of *Rights of Woman*—is in part due to the unconventional method of combining logic with aesthetic apprehension, and to her treatment of the arts not simply as the object of knowledge but as a medium of understanding. Her discourse is very different from that of Enlightenment predecessors like Locke or David Hume, or a contemporary such as Immanuel Kant. The manuscript 'Hints' include a reference to Kant's *Critique of Reason*, disputing his elevation of intellect over imagination:

> Mr. Kant has observed, that the understanding is sublime, the imagination beautiful—yet it is evident, that poets, and men who undoubtedly possess the liveliest imagination, are most touched by the sublime, while men who have cold, enquiring minds, have not this exquisite feeling in any great degree, and indeed seem to lose it as they cultivate their reason.

In her own writing she went further than Rousseau in combining close reasoning and lyricism, arguably anticipating the unconventional 19th-century thinkers Kierkegaard and Nietzsche.

Wollstonecraft did not fear the sleep of reason. On the contrary, in common with writers now labelled Gothic and Romantic, she was fascinated by madness, dreams, and nightmares as the manifestation of realms of experience and modes of expression beyond the limits of sober reason. At crisis points in her own life, especially those arising from the loss of a loved one through death or desertion, she records in her personal letters the dream visions that crowd in on her: Fanny Blood auguring death; Gilbert Imlay, with his unfixed identity, his 'different casts of countenance'. Her first novel, *Mary*, is in part a chronicle of the making of a romantic soul.

This semi-autobiographical fiction does not simply discuss the priority of imagination, the ability to envisage the unknown. It also performs it. We are told of the fictional Mary that, unhappy at home, she 'sought out a new world'. Surrounded by natural grandeur, sea, and mountains,

> Sublime ideas filled her young mind—always connected with devotional sentiments; extemporary effusions of gratitude, and rhapsodies of praise would burst often from her, when she listened to the birds, or pursued the deer. (ch. 2)

Later, having internalized the most celebrated pre-Romantic works of genius—the music of Handel, James Thomson's

The Seasons, and Edward Young's *Night-Thoughts* to supplement Shakespeare and Milton—she is driven to write down her rhapsodies. The results are woven into the text, intermingling the voices of heroine and narrator.

Commentators have sometimes belittled the stilted self-consciousness of this early work, but there is much to be learned from *Mary* about the high valuation Wollstonecraft placed on imagination, genius, and the aesthetics of the sublime in her final works. Wollstonecraft's last two major publications involved experimentation with a form of poetic prose. The *Letters Written During a Short Residence in Sweden, Norway and Denmark* drew the admiration of the Lake poets and had an influence on the evolution of the Romantic aesthetic. The novel fragment *The Wrongs of Woman: or, Maria*, too, can be seen as a vindication of the 'romantic' as a mode of being, a philosophical approach, and even as a practice of writing.

Letters Written During a Short Residence in Sweden, Norway and Denmark

In June 1795 Mary Wollstonecraft travelled to Scandinavia as the legal representative of her lover, the American entrepreneur Gilbert Imlay, father of her 1-year-old daughter Fanny. Her commission was to uncover the fate of a missing cargo of silver bullion and plate and the ship that carried it from revolutionary France to Norway, and to seek restoration or redress. During the three-month journey she wrote private letters to Imlay, which she requested back after their relationship finally ended in December. Godwin published 17 in redacted form in the 1798 *Posthumous Works*. The 25 letters in *A Short Residence*, which she published with Joseph Johnson in January 1796, recount the same tour, running the length of the coast from Gothenburg in Sweden westwards to the small fishing town of Risør in Norway and back, then down through Copenhagen into Germany (Figure 7). The letters she published in the travelogue differ considerably from the

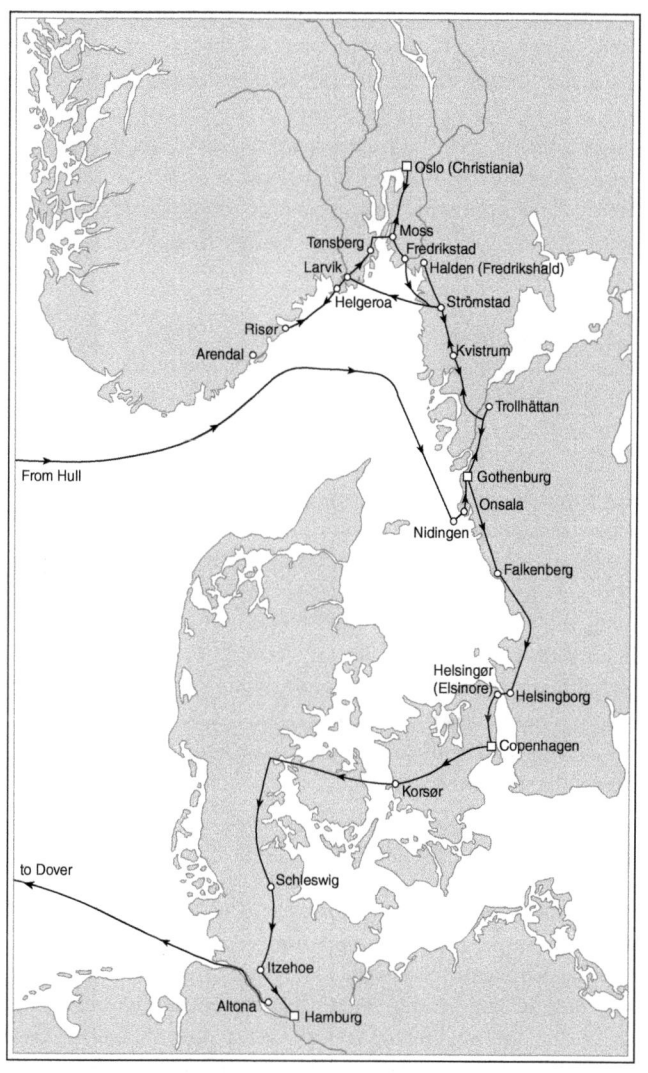

7. Mary Wollstonecraft's journey through Scandinavia, 1795.

original correspondence. They are addressed to an anonymous correspondent who is male and American, but the relationship to the writer remains unclear. In the travel book, apart from vague reference to 'affairs', the author gives no explanation for the curious itinerary. The final letter is signed 'Mary', but in large part the text is a literary construct that refers only indirectly to the nature of the enterprise, focusing instead on social and political observations, evocations of scenery, and the thoughts and emotions of the narrator.

Before departing from London, Wollstonecraft learned that Imlay had been unfaithful and that she and her daughter were facing abandonment. She felt this as an unbearable betrayal of the radical ideals that had brought them together. The private letters to Imlay are dominated by her anguished perplexity, as she struggles to find a way to understand their estrangement. What remains in the public letters is a colouring of bitter unexplained sorrow, just one facet of the changeable authorial persona. In *A Short Residence* she made full use of the versatility of travel-writing mode and the letter form to include a variety of voices, including the Enlightenment philosopher, the satirist, the disillusioned revolutionary, the irrepressible idealist, the connoisseur of the picturesque and sublime, and the original genius, with a prevailing mood of melancholy.

As with *A Vindication of the Rights of Woman*, the prefatory material is a good guide to the rationale of a complex work, and reveals the conscious craft of the writer. The short 'Advertisement' foregrounds the spontaneity of the writing. She will not simply describe, but let the commentary 'flow unrestrained' to record the effect on 'mind and feelings, whilst the impression was still fresh'. She does not apologize for the insistence on the personal: she is 'the little hero of each tale' (a joking quote from favourite poet Edward Young). Readers must decide for themselves whether 'they want to become better acquainted with me'.

Another major part of the plan, however, is 'simply to endeavour to give a just view of the present state of the countries I have passed through, as far as I could obtain information during so short a residence'. In almost every letter, she combines subjectivity and description with an analytical style of observation belonging to social science. Fact-finding and analysis were standard ingredients in 18th-century travel writing, though unorthodox when practised by a female author. Throughout the work, Wollstonecraft records information gleaned from English- or French-speaking rapporteurs. In Letter I she notes that a naval officer is paid 'little more than twelve pounds a year'. Over supper the man in question tells her 'bluntly that I was a woman of observation, for I asked him *men's questions*'.

Ever the educationalist, instruction remained a prime objective. As an Enlightenment thinker, she was interested in the big picture. The most northerly part of Europe remained little known in Britain, but the strategic importance of the region during the war with France increased curiosity. In each of the four countries she visited Wollstonecraft reflected on questions of historical development and national character. Initially she is unimpressed by the primitive conditions and mentality on the sparsely populated Swedish west coast. Later, as she passes through towns and cities and visits the homes of merchants and business-minded noblemen, her reflections become more nuanced. She weighs in the balance Rousseau's correlation of virtue and the savage state on the one hand and the progressivism of Adam Smith and the Scottish school on the other. Along the route, she investigates agricultural and industrial practices. Everywhere she is alert to signs of political reform and social progress. The letters address such topics as taxation and excise, property rights, crime and punishment, censorship and freedom of speech, class hierarchy, social manners and customs, the Denmark–Norway Union, and the impact of the assassination of Gustav III in Sweden. To a far greater extent than your average Enlightenment tour guide, because Wollstonecraft is a woman and a feminist, travelling in an all-female party with daughter Fanny and nursemaid Marguerite, she also looks at marriage laws and domestic life, women's work, and sexual mores, dwelling on the harsh treatment of English-born Queen Matilda of Denmark, accused of adultery.

Despite the range and tonal shifts of the text, from its first appearance certain readers framed *A Short Residence* as 'romantic' in the narrow sense: concerned with a doomed romance, and arousing amorous ideas through the presentation of a sensitive and vulnerable authorial persona. William Godwin claimed:

> ... a book of travels that so irresistibly seizes on the heart, never, in any other instance, found its way from the press. The occasional harshness and ruggedness of character, that diversify her Vindication of the Rights of Woman, here totally disappear. If ever there was a book calculated to make a man in love with its author, this appears to me to be the book. She speaks of her sorrows, in a way that fills us with melancholy, and dissolves us in tenderness, at the same time that she displays a genius which commands all our admiration. Affliction had tempered her heart to a softness almost more than human; and the gentleness of her spirit seems precisely to accord with all the romance of unbounded attachment. (ch. 8)

Godwin did go on to fall in love with the author within six months of publication, and eventually marry her. This assessment of the work appeared in the *Memoirs* he published shortly after her death. Compared with the 'masculine' *Rights of Woman*, he implies, the travelogue is a work that reinstates proper gender characteristics and operates on the male reader as a kind of invitation to desire. Other men in her circle, including the young poet Robert Southey and the playwright Thomas Holcroft, concurred.

When the biographer Richard Holmes paired *A Short Residence* with Godwin's *Memoirs* in an edition of 1987, he reinforced its reputation as the self-portrait of a 'passionate child of love'. Subsequent interpretations have provided a corrective, by examining intellectual content, such as cosmopolitanism, political economy, or nascent environmentalism, and taking into consideration Wollstonecraft's well-informed engagement with the genre of travel writing. She wrote a score of reviews of books of travel in *The Analytical Review* before attempting to write one, and took a keen interest in the porous and dynamic nature of the category. In the review of *Letters concerning the northern Coast of the County of Antrim*, she remarked, 'The art of travelling is only a branch of the art of thinking.'

When Wollstonecraft recast the letters to Imlay in the form of a travelogue designed for the public, she substantially curtailed the autobiographical material. Consequently, although *A Short Residence* hints at disappointed love and the attempt to move beyond it, this strand is a subset of a more comprehensive quest narrative. The work is 'romantic' in the sense of idealistic. Hope is the treasure the narrator seeks. She has been crushed not only by personal loss, but by the experience of watching at first hand the universal promise of the French Revolution unravel. The business side of the mission was a limited success; the captain was interviewed, the ship found and refurbished, and Wollstonecraft wrote to the Danish prime minister in an attempt to further the legal process. In contrast, the journey as a mode of philosophical enquiry and imaginative stimulus revived her sense of purpose.

For Wollstonecraft, lived experience is *the* matter of philosophy and, as a consequence, her philosophical ideas are constantly evolving. Letter I dramatizes the process. The narrator and her two companions are dropped at random on a rocky shore. Before long, they are welcomed with kindness into the home of the coastguard and his family; she is transported by the silent grandeur of the coast, the signs of growth amid the giant rocks, the midnight sun, casting an enchanted stillness over nature, and the sight of her infant daughter's calm slumber. These impressions mixed with 'the idea of home' and 'reflections on the state of society' provoke ambiguous emotions and sharpen her sensations. She feels 'more alive than usual':

> What are these imperious sympathies? How frequently has melancholy and even mysanthropy taken possession of me, when the world has disgusted me, and friends have proved unkind. I have then considered myself as a particle broken off from the grand mass of mankind;—I was alone, till some involuntary sympathetic emotion, like the attraction of adhesion, made me feel that I was still a part of a mighty whole, from which I could not sever myself—not, perhaps, for the reflection has been carried very far, by snapping the thread of an existence which loses charms in proportion as the cruel experience of life stops or poisons the current of the heart. (Letter I)

This passage, believed to have inspired Coleridge's poem 'Frost at Midnight', adapts the associationist psychology of David Hartley to reflect on reasons for continuing to be, and the conditions of faith in a better world. Reveries of this kind led Godwin to dub his late wife 'a female Werter'. The hero of Goethe's novella *The Sorrows of Young Werther* (1774) was one of the icons of Romantic literary sensibility, a figure in whom an immense capacity for happiness is matched by abyssal depths of pain that ultimately lead to suicide. Hamlet's question 'to be or not to be' echoes subtly through *A Short Residence*. One of her destinations is Elsinore in Denmark, the location of Shakespeare's play.

It was the agonizing deterioration of the relationship with Gilbert Imlay that led Wollstonecraft to forge a more assertive concept of the 'romantic', in contrast to the self-interested materialism he represented. In private letters to him she constantly probed a dichotomy carried over into the travel book. 'I will allow you to cultivate my judgment,' she wrote in August 1794, 'if you will permit me to keep alive the sentiments in your heart, which may be termed romantic ... the offspring of the senses and the imagination ...' The following month, when he was on business in London and she forlorn in Paris with their infant, she evolved a new philosophy of the imagination, cancelling her previous position in *Rights of Men* that reason is what lifts humans above the animal world, towards perfectibility:

> Believe me, sage sir, you have not sufficient respect for the imagination—I could prove to you in a trice that it is the mother of sentiment, the great distinction of our nature, the only purifier of the passions—animals have a portion of reason, and equal, if not more exquisite, senses; but no trace of imagination, or her offspring taste, appears in any of their actions.

Reason may draw humans together, she adds, but 'imagination is the true fire, stolen from heaven, to animate this cold creature of clay, producing all those fine sympathies that lead to rapture, rendering men social by expanding their hearts'. Combatively she concludes, 'if you call these observations romantic I shall be apt to retort, that you are embruted by trade and the vulgar enjoyments of life'.

Her version of imagination is future orientated, distinct both from the reactionary extravagances of Edmund Burke, idealizing feudal times, and from Rousseau's backward-looking concept of the state of nature, the 'golden age of stupidity' as Wollstonecraft called it (Letter IX). Although she admires the 'romantic views' of the northern wilderness, she maintains that clearance of forests will bring prosperity and thereby the unfolding of human faculties. Imagination provides the incentive for change, an impulse towards improvement consolidated by reflection, judgement, and reason. At the same time strong imagination is a wayward force, informed by emotion. At one stage, while sailing along a wild coast, imagination overleaps itself and carries her ideas forward by millennia, presenting her with visions of future famine and the misery of 'fellow creatures yet unborn' when nature has been entirely depleted by excessive cultivation (Letter XI). At another, having heard stories of 'golden age' virtues in the far north, imagination tempts her 'to seek an asylum in such a retreat from all the disappointments I am threatened with; but reason drags me back, whispering that the world is still the world, and man the same compound of weakness and folly' (Letter XIV). Imagination is, despite everything, the cure for rationalist cynicism, 'the only solace for the feeling heart', a capacity which makes it possible to continue living and adhering to others (Letter X).

A distinctive feature of Wollstonecraft's tour, the companionship of her infant daughter 'Fannikin', roots it in feminism and futurity (Letter XII). A plot within the plot of the travelogue is the oscillation of separation and reunion, hope and despair in relation to her child. Maternal feeling gives rise to intellectual realization, informed by the political analysis of women's condition. As in the reveries of Letter I, the child is often unconsciously the author of philosophical reflection.

There is an echo of the concern expressed in *Vindication of the Rights of Woman*, when she asks, invoking Milton's picture of hell, 'would it not be a refinement on cruelty' to open the mind of a girl only 'to make the darkness and misery of her fate *visible*?' (ch. 5). Regarding Fanny, the narrator of *Short Residence* feels 'more than a mother's fondness and anxiety, when I reflect on the dependent and oppressed state of her sex'. She dreads to 'cultivate sensibility' and 'unfold her mind, lest it should render her unfit for the world she is to inhabit—Hapless woman! what a fate is thine!' (Letter VI)

In one of the final letters from *Short Residence*, anticipating a sceptical response to her musings on the tragic fate of Queen Matilda of Denmark, her feminist analysis dissolves the dichotomy of reason and feeling: 'Still harping on the same subject, you will exclaim—How can I avoid it, when most of the struggles of an eventful life have been occasioned by the oppressed state of my sex? They reason deeply, who strongly feel' (Letter XIX). Her style of writing, mixing literary allusion, autobiographical confession, and philosophical argument, itself points to an idiosyncratic and innovative form of knowledge-making, stemming from an area of concerns now classified as aesthetic: genius, imagination, taste.

The lengthy title of the Scandinavian travelogue is often shortened to *Letters from Sweden*, but the words 'A Short Residence' are thematically important. From the first page there is recurrent emphasis on the idea of home, the forming of new attachments that are then torn apart, feelings of belonging or isolation. The climax of the account is a month-long sojourn in Tønsberg in Norway, when legal delays forced Wollstonecraft to pause. During this idyll, she walked on the coastal paths, learned to row, bathed in the sea, and formed friendships with some of the local women. Her health and hopes revived. The town came to seem 'something like home' (Letter XII). But a letter from Imlay received on the way back to rejoin Fanny and Marguerite in Gothenberg shattered her peace of mind. In one of her original letters to him, from Copenhagen, she wrote: 'I am weary of travelling—yet seem to have no home—no resting place to look to—I am strangely cast off.' *A Short Residence* ends on the same note: 'I am weary of changing the scene, and quitting people and places the moment they begin to interest me' (Letter XXV). On landing at Dover, the voice of the narrator fades out as she wanders solitary around 'this dirty place, literally, to kill time'.

The Wrongs of Woman: or, Maria

Maria is a romantic. That is both her problem and the solution to it. This characteristic traps her in the miseries of the status quo, but also motivates her rebellion against it. In the 'Author's Preface' to *Wrongs of Woman*, Wollstonecraft draws attention to the experimental nature of the flawed heroine. The eponymous heroine, like the main protagonist of the novel *Mary* and the narrator in *Short Residence*, is a questing, questioning figure, modelling a female selfhood possessing reason, passion, and imagination in an unstable amalgam.

Here, as in *Mary*, the heroine has been shaped by the natural environment. 'Born in one of the most romantic parts of England', Maria writes in a memoir addressed to her daughter, her intense love of nature gave rise to her first reflections and inspired a 'pleasure that employed and formed my imagination'. The second major influence was her uncle, an administrator who had gained a fortune in India but then, disappointed in love, retired from the world. From him she learns habits of ardent expression and moral independence that equally serve to feed her imagination and help explain 'some peculiarities in my character, which by the world are indefinitely termed romantic' (ch. 7).

To an extent *Wrongs of Woman* is autobiographical, though Maria's circumstances differ in many respects. Wollstonecraft's object, as in *Mary*, was to examine and dramatize the impact of oppression on the state of mind of a thinking woman. The main title indicates not just the reverse of the *Rights of Woman*, but also a philosophical aim by way of fictional illustration, as explained in the 'Author's Preface'. The condition of 'woman' will be addressed, not simply the history 'of an individual', in order to show 'the misery and oppression, peculiar to women, that arise out of the partial laws and customs of society'. The ambiguous statement that follows, 'The sentiments I have embodied', suggests both the source in the being of the author and the way fictional devices of plot and character are used to externalize disregarded psychological and emotional evils of various kinds. The name of the rule-breaking Maria is foregrounded in the subtitle, but an even greater novelty was the creation of a second heroine, the working-class survivor of trauma, Jemima, who relates her own life story, alongside vignettes featuring the voices of other working women.

Wollstonecraft redeemed the promise of a second volume of *Rights of Woman* focused on law, with a narrative in which the consequences of legal and economic inequality come to the fore. The narrative dramatizes coverture, the doctrine that a wife's legal being is suspended and absorbed into that of her husband and that she is subject to his authority. It touches on child custody rights, married women's property, domestic abuse, divorce, and, beyond marriage, women's experience of discrimination and sexual violence in the workplace.

When the pregnant Maria escapes her profligate husband, who had attempted to pimp her to a rich creditor, he issues a newspaper advertisement stating that his wife had 'without any assignable cause, absconded from her husband; and any person harbouring her, was menaced with the utmost severity of the law' (ch. 12). A landlady, fearful of the threat, tells Maria her parallel story of financial abuse by her errant husband, concluding 'women have always the worst of it, when law is to decide' (ch. 13). The incident expands on Maria's previous reflection that a mother 'cannot *lawfully*' prevent a 'gambling spendthrift, or beastly drunkard' of a husband from seizing and spending a wife's inheritance or earnings while, conversely,

> the laws of her country—if women have a country—afford her no
> protection or redress from the oppressor, unless she have the plea of
> bodily fear; yet how many ways are there of goading the soul almost
> to madness, equally unmanly, though not so mean? (ch. 11)

It was the attempt to communicate the experience of a 'soul almost goaded to madness' or to suicidal despair that led Wollstonecraft to clothe her sentiments in fictional form.

According to William Godwin as posthumous editor, she found it no easy task. Usually a speedy and sure-footed writer, she struggled with the design of the plot for 12 months, constantly rewriting, and before she died had only reached the halfway point, leaving drafts of 17 chapters in different states of completion.

The composition of the novel coincided with the development of Wollstonecraft's relationship with Godwin. They became lovers in August 1796, Wollstonecraft found she was pregnant by December, and in March 1797 they decided on marriage, in spite of their mutual, outspoken dislike of the institution. He had established a name as author of the anarchist treatise *Political Justice* (1793) and the popular novel *Caleb Williams* (1794). It was his practice to submit work-in-progress to friends, and he urged her to do the same. In spring of 1797, she offered a version of the opening chapters to Godwin and his friend George Dyson, translator of *The Sorcerer*, a fashionable imported German horror novel. Both found the heroine's wrongs relatively trivial and urged her to heighten 'incidents'. Godwin warned that she should avoid 'a commonplace story of a brutal insensible husband'. Wollstonecraft replied to Dyson that 'she was vexed and surprised' at his 'not thinking the situation of Maria sufficiently important' and could 'only account for this want of—shall I say it? delicacy of feeling, by recollecting that you are a man'. She insisted on the seriousness of the pain endured by a 'woman of sensibility' chained intimately to a tyrant, 'yet you do not seem to be disgusted with him!!!'

Godwin published the politer part of the letter to Dyson as an 'Author's Preface', a manifesto for her approach to political and philosophical fiction:

> These appear to me (matrimonial despotism of heart and conduct) to be the peculiar Wrongs of Woman, because they degrade the mind. What are termed great misfortunes, may more forcibly impress the minds of common readers; they have more of what

may justly be termed *stage-effect* but it is the delineation of finer sensations which, in my opinion, constitutes the merit of our best novels, this is what I have in view…

Nevertheless, like other authors of so-called 'Jacobin Novels' in her set, she wanted her political agenda to reach a wide and varied audience, and accepted the need to come up with a compelling plot line. She revised the structure of the first volume, and left multiple and varying 'scattered heads for the continuation of the story' that Godwin put in the editorial conclusion. The fourth consisted simply of: 'Divorced by her husband—Her lover unfaithful—Pregnancy—Miscarriage—Suicide'. She reread Godwin's *Caleb Williams*, which opposes class hierarchy by means of a pursuit narrative of almost supernatural ferocity, and studied the way he joined his radical message to elements of the 1790s trend for tales of terror. Among the Gothic plot devices she borrowed were incarceration and legal persecution, featuring two fugitives, for both Maria and Jemima learn what it is to be outcasts and outlaws.

Despite the dismissal of '*stage-effect*' in the letter to Dyson, Wollstonecraft eventually hit upon the perfect *coup de théâtre* for her opening page. Maria awakens from a drugged stupor into an incomprehensible nightmare, crazed with grief at separation from her infant girl, struggling to separate reality from fantasy, surrounded by the shrieks of maniacs. The lines are a tribute to the celebrated Ann Radcliffe and her spectral tales of persecuted heroines, a mode called at the time 'modern romance', but they also convey the message, 'I am describing the real world, and the real world far surpasses the imaginary horrors of the Gothic.' The reader, too, is disorientated, seeking explanations that will not come until many chapters later. Maria's husband George Venables has taken custody of their child and imprisoned Maria herself in a private madhouse, as is his legal right. The symbolism is apparent from the outset. Maria asks herself if there is a point to attempting escape or nurturing a daughter: 'Was not the world a vast prison, and women born slaves?' (ch. 1). The true horror is awareness of the intangible prison constructed of the 'partial laws enacted by men'. In the memoir written for her lost child, Maria declares, 'Marriage has bastilled me for life' (ch. 10). The Bastille may have fallen in 1789, but there was no prospect of liberation for the female sex.

While Maria is not yet mad, faced with this injustice her imaginative faculties become toxic, and in isolation her romantic nature begins to lead her astray. A warning appears in the form of a 'lovely maniac' in the neighbouring cell who sings a ballad of surpassing sweetness, but whose reason has been destroyed by a forced marriage and postpartum depression. Without employment, Maria passes the time reading books borrowed from another prisoner with the assistance of the increasingly sympathetic guard Jemima. Under the influence of the novel *La Nouvelle Héloïse* by the great seducer Rousseau, 'treacherous fancy' leads Maria to transform the unknown lender, one Henry Darnford, into a heroic saviour. She herself reflects on 'how difficult it was for women to avoid growing romantic' when 'there is nothing to divert the mind' (ch. 2). Later we will learn that she suffered similar delusions when, desperate to leave the prison of her father's house, she looked to Venables, on slight evidence, as a rescuer and safe harbour.

So far, the narrative seems in line with criticism of excessive sensibility as a female weakness in *Rights of Woman*. The impression is reinforced when Darnford and Maria eventually meet and he relates his life story to Maria in a style of flattering gallantry. A former British officer who became a friend of American liberty, he is also a self-confessed libertine who transfers the blame to women of ill repute. Maria's mind has been 'softened' by idleness; she is trapped by 'romantic wishes', 'romantic expectations', and pity into letting his self-justifications pass (ch. 4). Here the term 'romantic' pivots towards error, but Maria is not condemned in the analysis that follows. The narrator condones the blend of sensuality, sensibility, idealism, and trust in the character, and ends with praise of the imagination as the basis for hope.

Jemima is drawn into the atmosphere of trust, and tells her own story to Maria and Darnford. It is one of the most remarkable passages in 18th-century fiction, a break with the sentimental tradition of lost innocence and unmerited woe, as practised in works by other sympathetic female reformers, such as Elizabeth Inchbald and Mary Hays. The idiom is naked truth, with a remarkable level of documentary detail while, at the same time, Jemima provides an incisive critical commentary on her own history in a style similar to the authorial voice in *Rights of Woman*, or to Maria in her more philosophical moments. This bleak account devoid of illusions is an implicit rebuke to the prejudices not only of Darnford, but also of Maria, who had beforehand written in her memoir that her husband's crass vulgarity reminded her of viewing the 'squalid inhabitants' of the city back streets, 'mortified to consider them as my fellow creatures' (ch. 12). Now Maria takes Jemima's hand in fellow feeling. This act of communion sparks Jemima's imaginative ability to hope, while in Maria it temporarily suspends hope by making 'her thoughts take a wider range' to encompass 'the oppressed state of women' and consider the outlook for her own unprotected lost daughter. The two women will make common cause and escape the madhouse. It would seem from the fragment of a conclusion that they are destined to share a future, though Jemima insists on retaining her economic independence in the position of paid housekeeper.

Later narrative developments eventually reframe Maria's 'romantic' attachment to Darnford. The heroine's memoir shows the way the false step in marrying Venables was inextricably tied to her compassion and faith in humanity. The fact that her husband comes to ridicule her for 'the folly of romantic sentiments' proves the point that 'romantic' stands for far more than escapist illusion. It represents an alternative standard of morality based on the vision of a world that does not exist, that can only be imagined; a time when women are free. Most radically, the novel insists that women's sexual feelings are a vital part of this freedom. Even if Godwin's *Memoirs* had never been written, the memoir of Maria Venables in *Wrongs of Woman* was demonstration enough of the author's outrageous immorality for conventional moralists. Maria relates explicitly her increasing disgust at sexual intercourse with her husband, her regret at submitting against her wishes, leading to pregnancy, and her final refusal after his attempt to barter her emerges. When she states that she intends to leave him she is confined to her bedchamber. She opens a window and experiences a strange imaginative premonition of liberty:

> The face of heaven grew fairer as I viewed it, and the clouds seemed to flit away obedient to my wishes, to give my soul room to expand. I was all soul, and (wild as it may appear) felt as if I could have dissolved in the soft balmy gale that kissed my cheek, or have glided below the horizon on the glowing, descending beams. (ch. 11)

It is an 'emancipation of the mind', an epiphany at once divine and sensual, and an affirmation of moral autonomy even into the most jealously guarded realm of male-dominated society, control of women's sexuality. She is 'disgusted' by the way 'novelists and moralists praise as a virtue' women's willingness to submit to sex without love. Such women may be good 'in the ordinary acceptation of the phrase', but they do so at the expense of truth. They lack 'that fire of the imagination, which produces *active* sensibility, and *positive* virtue' (ch. 10). Such an unfiltered letter from mother to daughter might be improbable, but Wollstonecraft was addressing all her political daughters, and looking towards a time when 'false refinement' would no longer deny their needs and wants, in addition to rejecting their civil and political rights.

It is for this reason that, after escaping the lunatic asylum, Maria does not renounce her illicit relationship with Darnford, even when she has a more realistic idea of his qualities and limitations. Instead, she follows through on her convictions as a free moral agent and returns to London, living with him in open defiance of the rules of decorum, in spite of rejection by former friends and legal threats from her husband.

After Maria's memoir ends, the surviving section of the narrative culminates in a court case. Darnford is prosecuted for 'criminal conversation', a charge deriving from the doctrine of coverture, treating the wife as stolen property and requiring financial damages from the male seducer to the husband. Maria insists on facing 'the dogs of law' directly. She orders the defence counsel 'to plead guilty to the charge of adultery; but to deny that of seduction'; a feminist distinction. Although debarred from court in person, she writes testimony to be read aloud. In this impassioned statement, she describes the aggravating circumstances in her individual case, while also taking a public stand against the wrongs experienced by women at the hands of the law. She demands a divorce (no wife in England had ever been granted one), on the basis of her husband's cruelties, and the right to choose a new partner. The narrator comments: 'The sarcasms of society and the condemnation of a mistaken world, were nothing to her, compared with acting contrary to those feelings which were the foundation of her principles' (ch. 17).

The judge in his summing up inevitably denounces 'the fallacy of letting women please their feelings, as an excuse for the violation of the marriage-vow...What virtuous woman thought of her feelings?—It was her duty to love and obey the man chosen by her parents and relations.' Incarceration was admittedly a severe measure, but hereditary insanity 'might render that however a prudent measure; and indeed the conduct of the lady did not appear that of a person of sane mind' (ch. 17). And so the narrative comes full circle, and the analogy of the madhouse and society at large is confirmed. Since the world will not allow such a woman as Maria to exist, she logically turns to suicide in an apparent re-enactment of Wollstonecraft's own attempt by laudanum overdose in May 1795. Yet the author's characteristic mode of romantic optimism would seemingly not allow her to end the story there, and in a final fragment of connected text the heroine is revived by the last-minute intervention of her companion Jemima, with rescued daughter, and the mother resolves to live for her child. Tragically, it became Wollstonecraft's final word to posterity.

Mary Wollstonecraft

Chapter 6
Reintroducing Mary Wollstonecraft

Until the 1970s the writings of Mary Wollstonecraft were little known because they were unavailable. If she was discussed at all, it was because of biographies that tended to follow the template devised by William Godwin, emphasizing the life story at the expense of the works. With the advent of the women's liberation movement, the trickle of biographical studies became a torrent, pressure grew from women's studies specialists to add her writings to the university curriculum, and paperback editions of the *Vindications*, the novels, and extracts from other works became available.

It was only in 1989 that the full range of her publications became accessible outside rare book collections in university libraries. There is a case for saying that previous generations of readers barely knew Wollstonecraft. The seven-volume edition of her works, edited by Janet Todd and Marilyn Butler, for the first time revealed a complete picture of her 10-year career as author. It supplemented the core texts—the two political *Vindications*, the two novels, and the Scandinavian travelogue—with a dozen more. A volume was dedicated to over 400 newly identified reviews from the *Analytical Review*. This allowed the replacement of vague references to hack work with a new map of Wollstonecraft's affiliations and antipathies within the literary marketplace of her era. Areas of enquiry that have expanded as a result of the edition include Wollstonecraft as educationalist, Wollstonecraft as translator, Wollstonecraft as journalist and book critic, and Wollstonecraft as historian of the French Revolution. As Virginia Sapiro remarked in a review of the edition, 'Too little attention has been paid to the range of Wollstonecraft's writing, and perhaps therefore too much silliness written about it.' The outlines of the life became legible as the chronology of a writing career.

Change came in the early 1990s in the form of systematic assessment of Wollstonecraft's contributions to education theory, literature, philosophy, and political science. Better availability of all the works accelerated and consolidated change by offering readers and scholars a body of evidence detached from and exceeding in many ways the long-dominant source for the interpretation of her life and ideas, Godwin's *Memoirs*. The restoration of the corpus has begun to displace his account of the life.

Mary Wollstonecraft died on 10 September 1797, 10 days after giving birth to her second daughter, Mary. The child survived and was raised in Godwin's household with her older half-sister Fanny; she would go on to win fame as the author of *Frankenstein*, among many other publications, and as wife, collaborator, and editor of the poet Percy Bysshe Shelley. The mother was buried on 15 September in the graveyard of St Pancras Old Church, where she and William Godwin had married five months earlier. Godwin did not attend the funeral. He was already channelling his intense grief into writing a biography that would bear testament to her greatness of spirit and capacity for love, while preparing some of her unpublished papers for publication. Their relationship had lasted only a year. Many aspects of her life were unknown to him. He made enquiries to fill gaps, but would not wait for cooperation from her sisters, who were anxious to prevent scandalous revelations. They were right to fear the result. Godwin resolved to outface moralists by emphasizing and even rhapsodizing upon liaisons out of wedlock with Henry Fuseli,

Gilbert Imlay, and himself. His strategy included publishing her tortured letters to Imlay as exemplars of amatory literature. Impervious to the way they would be seized on as evidence of her immorality, he presented Wollstonecraft herself as a victim of passion.

Both the *Memoirs* and the *Posthumous Works* appeared at the start of 1798. Wollstonecraft was described in both titles as '*the Author of A Vindication of the Rights of Woman*'. Yet Godwin's familiarity with her writings was incomplete and his appraisals were skewed by a preference for confessional works like the early novel *Mary* and the Scandinavian *Letters*, and ambivalence regarding the 'masculine' and 'rugged' *Rights of Woman*. One of Wollstonecraft's former colleagues reviewed the *Memoirs* anonymously in the *Analytical Review*, and observed that while the narrative account was touching and true as far as it went, it failed to trace the development of the subject's intellect and opinions: 'It gives us no correct history of her favourite books, her hours of study, nor her attainments in languages and philosophy.' This was consequential, the reviewer explained, because it obscured the rational principles behind her actions.

Godwin's lack of discretion about Wollstonecraft's private life has been condemned from that day to this. One of her contemporary admirers, the poet Robert Southey, complained that Godwin showed 'the want of all feeling in stripping his dead wife naked, as he did'. Gillian Ayres, in a 2017 study of Wollstonecraft biographies, states, 'by writing the *Memoirs*, he effectively buried his wife for the next two hundred years by telling the world that she had attempted suicide twice and conceived two children out of wedlock'. He has been held responsible for setting back the influence of her feminist ideas. His disclosures seemed especially perverse in view of his remark in chapter 9 of the *Memoirs* that their decision to marry when Mary was four months pregnant was due to the fact that she 'had an extreme aversion to be made the topic of vulgar discussion'.

A problem with this view is that it downplays Wollstonecraft's own reckless disregard for her reputation at every turn. When she wrote to Everina in November 1787 announcing that she intended to live by writing, she knew this step would expose her to 'ridicule'. As early as *Thoughts on the Education of Daughters*, her first book, she declaimed against 'false shame', observing, 'How many people are like whitened sepulchres, and careful only about appearances! yet if we are too anxious to gain the approbation of the world, we must often forfeit our own.' The novel *Mary* maintained the theme of contempt for those whose minds are 'shackled with a set of notions concerning propriety'. The heroine reveals to a near stranger with her 'usual frankness' her revulsion against her husband.

Later, as Wollstonecraft pursued her ever more unorthodox course through life, she frequently expressed in letters her indifference to scandal and asserted an independent measure of morality. She shrugged when people stared at the evidence of her first pregnancy or (Archibald Hamilton Rowan reminisced) the sight of her 'parading' about Paris with 'a child at her heels' and no known husband. At the end of her relationship with Imlay she assured him that his reputation would not suffer by leaving her, as she 'never concealed the nature of my connection with you'. After her attempted suicide by drowning in October 1795 she told him it was 'one of the calmest acts of reason' and denied that it was motivated by fear of public opprobrium following his desertion: 'Did I care for what is called reputation, it is by other circumstances that I should be dishonoured.' In setting him free from all obligations, including financial support for their child, she stated, 'I fear neither poverty nor infamy.' This stance involved apparent carelessness regarding the future of young Fanny, as well as her own intellectual bequest. She added in explanation, 'My child may have to blush for her mother's want of prudence—may lament that the rectitude of my heart made me above vulgar precautions; but she shall not despise me for meanness.' When she married Godwin in March 1797, exposing her previous unmarried status, and was socially ostracized by several in her circle, she replied to a letter from Amelia Alderson expressing her 'indignant contempt for the forms of a world'. The refusal to compromise with public opinion and insistence on acting according to her own principles was an important feature of her radicalism.

It is further evidence in defence of Godwin's candour that elements in her unfinished novel *The Wrongs of Woman*, published in the *Posthumous Works*, were as explosive as anything in the *Memoirs*. Wollstonecraft's reflections on rape, abortion, prostitution, marriage, adultery, and divorce were sufficiently sensational in themselves to draw the attention of critics to controversial aspects of the author's life and conduct.

Had she lived, she would in any case have found it increasingly difficult to gain a hearing for her ideas on the equality of the sexes. In the immediate aftermath of Wollstonecraft's death, several admirers, including Mary Hays, Mary Robinson, Mary Anne Radcliffe, and Priscilla Wakefield, took up her mantle in polemical treatises and political novels. Significantly, they published polemics without putting their name on the title page: a sign of the increasingly high stakes of publicly espousing the cause of women. The next few decades were marked by ever more reactionary politics in Europe, including France, matched by deepening opposition to social experiments, including in the areas of family law and of women's rights, education, and opportunities for employment. Successful mainstream writers with a duty to maintain respectability, like the acclaimed novelists Frances Burney and Maria Edgeworth, helped to sustain the ideal of female agency while distancing themselves by presenting extreme feminist caricatures in their novels. The niche author Jane Austen subtly smuggled terminology from *Rights of Woman* into *Pride and Prejudice*, where Elizabeth Bennet demands to be treated as a 'rational creature'. While there was no sudden halt to the spread of Wollstonecraft's ideas in Britain and beyond, very often they were presented with strategic indirection.

The failure to establish and maintain traditions of feminist thought is the norm up to the late 20th century. The press was male dominated, female education remained sporadic, and a critical mass of target readers was slow to emerge. Just as the early feminist philosopher Mary Astell was forgotten by the time Mary Wollstonecraft and other radical thinkers started to reflect on the rights and wrongs of woman a century later, so Wollstonecraft's legacy was often obscured and remained only partially accessible in the coming years. She herself anticipated this when she commented in *Vindication of the Rights of Woman* on the power of dominant ideology:

> Men and women must be educated, in a great degree by the opinions and manners of the society they live in. In every age there has been a stream of popular opinion that has carried all before it, and given a family character, as it were, to the century. It may then fairly be inferred, that, till society is differently constituted, much cannot be expected from education. (ch. 2)

A number of streams of 'popular opinion' shaped the reception of Wollstonecraft from the 19th century to the present.

Knowledge of the life and work initially narrowed to *A Vindication of the Rights of Woman* and Godwin's *Memoirs*, the two texts offering polar opposite versions of Wollstonecraft from which to select. George Eliot in a journal article of 1855 omits mention of the latter and was able to report with delight that in *Rights of Woman* the 'grave pages are lit up by no ray of fancy'. It is a sober, earnest work, she continues, entirely in conformity with Victorian notions of female domesticity and service. Eliot adopted Wollstonecraft's point that men too suffered from the skewed relations created when women are driven to gain power through sexual allure, the only means available, and eventually illustrated it in her picture of the union of failed idealist Dr Lydgate and the coquette Rosamond Vincy in *Middlemarch* (1871–2). Others would endorse Wollstonecraft's pragmatic remarks on education and women's higher duties within marriage, as well as her hints towards the political franchise and greater scope for economic independence, but they found her unflattering descriptions of fine ladies absorbed by trivia a stumbling block. Those who championed the cause of women in the period tended to do so by praising feminine domestic virtues and asserting innate moral superiority, rather than by appealing to the capacity for reason shared by men and women. The language of 'rights' failed to chime.

While in the Victorian era Godwin's *Memoirs* remained a liability, a portrait to be exonerated in sympathetic biographical sketches by Anne Elwood (1843) and C. Kegan Paul (1876, 1879), at the end of the century it became a resource for the New Woman generation who rejected marital dependence and embraced sexual emancipation. The anarchist Emma Goldman in an essay of 1911 hailed Wollstonecraft as a fearless pioneer in the realm of social and sexual mores. Wollstonecraft, she argues, aimed at inner liberation beyond 'external gains' such as the vote, though at a tragic cost. Focusing exclusively on biography, Goldman concluded: 'Had Mary Wollstonecraft not written a line, her life would have furnished food for thought.' Virginia Woolf similarly disregarded the substance of the writings when in 1929 she wrote her inspired tribute to Wollstonecraft the experimentalist, simply observing that the *Vindications* 'are so true that they seem now to contain nothing new in them—their originality has become our commonplace'.

Woolf's conclusion, that the wild wishes of Wollstonecraft had become the new normal, was exposed as fanciful optimism during the anti-feminist backlash following the Second World War. Still relying on Godwin's *Memoirs*, an American best-selling diatribe *Modern Woman: The Lost Sex* (1947), written by journalist Ferdinand Lundberg and psychiatrist Marynia Farnham with the aim of driving women from the workforce, presented Mary Wollstonecraft as the origin of the conjuncture of feminism and neurosis. Their summary of the tenets of *A Vindication of the*

Rights of Woman indicated that they had never opened it. Instead, Godwin's account of her unhappy childhood led to the diagnosis that 'Wollstonecraft hated men', with the elaboration that she was 'an extreme neurotic of a compulsive type' whose disorder forced her to compete aggressively in a masculine sphere while masochistically abasing herself towards unreliable lovers. *Modern Woman* had a progressive effect by provoking Betty Friedan to write *The Feminine Mystique* (1963), often credited with launching the second wave feminist movement.

The slogan 'The personal is political' appeared to match perfectly the story of Wollstonecraft's life and critical awakening. As it resounded through lecture halls, rallies, and protest marches in the 1970s, new biographies of the 'first feminist' appeared every year. She had tenaciously attempted to give meaning to the disparate raw material of her experience through the activity of writing, and gradually it assumed shape and focus as part of a wider social critique of the structures of oppression. Nearly 200 years later, the process of drawing feminist inference from personal experience became a mass, collective phenomenon.

The swing of the pendulum between the influence of the *Memoirs* and the *Rights of Woman* ceased as both became better known and moral codes relaxed. Still the apparent contradictions in the two works represented a puzzle. Was Wollstonecraft a champion of reason, a bourgeois forerunner to 'liberal feminism' with its relatively limited agenda of equality through reform of legal and political structures? Or was she an instinctive radical, without a systematic analysis or set of objectives, whose importance lay in the example of her fearless resistance to social discrimination? Knowledge of the whole span of her writings and reflections, and serious engagement with her contribution to Enlightenment political philosophy, broke this deadlock.

In the 21st century, there has been a phenomenal deepening and broadening in the understanding of Wollstonecraft as a historical figure. And yet in many ways, she seems to defy the laws of historical gravity. It has turned out that she, of all the radical Romantics, is the one who most stubbornly refuses to die, or be pinned down to a historical moment. Somehow Wollstonecraft's preoccupations and experimental modes of expression continue to speak intelligibly to present-day crises and debates. It is as if she is part of a war of ideas that has not yet ended.

Events have vindicated literary scholar Cora Kaplan's prediction in 2002 that we would not have the luxury of calmly assessing Wollstonecraft's legacy from the perspective of a 'postfeminist utopia', but would find ourselves still enmeshed in the problems and questions that she addressed. In spite of a patchwork of levelling legislation and efforts to establish an egalitarian consensus, a *longue durée* of female subordination continues globally. As news headlines announce the failures and rollback of equality between the sexes over the first decades of the 21st century, the impression is not that she was ahead of her time but instead that we remain in her time, and her terms of reference are not alien to present-day struggles.

Wollstonecraft had faith in the future. She frequently wrote of feeling out of step with the customs and prejudices of her society, and expected to be vindicated by the progress of generations to come. Her creed of perfectibility led her to state in the Introduction to *Rights of Woman*, 'Rousseau exerts himself to prove, that all *was* right originally: a crowd of authors that all *is* now right: and I, that all *will be* right.'

It must be admitted that sometimes she called it wrong. Much as she worshipped God in nature, when touring the wild Scandinavian coast with its vast stretches of woodland she is very much the anthropocentric Enlightenment philosopher. In *Letters Written During a Short Residence in Sweden, Norway and Denmark* she predicted, 'The destruction, or gradual reduction, of the forests, will probably meliorate the climate', and added to her correspondent, 'I never, my friend, thought so deeply of the advantages obtained by human industry as since I have been in Norway. The world requires, I see, the hand of man to perfect it...' (Letter X). These remarks are part of a class-based critique; she objected to the monopolizing of natural resources by the wealthy. They can be explained historically, but they have not aged well.

Wollstonecraft took an internationalist approach to the problem of women's oppression. *Rights of Woman* was among other things an intervention to ameliorate the condition of women in France, and during her sojourn in Paris she witnessed the political activism of working-class women at first hand. In *Short Residence* she examined the lives of women of all conditions in the Nordic region. Increasingly she aimed to account for the differential effect of patriarchy as refracted by economics and class. However her analysis stops short at race, and the analogy she makes between the state of white European women and slavery, although rooted in classical tradition and legal definitions, can be described retrospectively as insensitive at the very least, employed at a time when colonial slavery was at its height and a topic of heated debate. She condemned the slave trade forcefully, but other writers, notably other women writers, did more to argue the case. Failure to address difference and acknowledge the divergent experiences and wrongs of non-European peoples was a blot on most Enlightenment thinking, and this failure fed into racist ideology. Alternatively the moral universals of the Enlightenment, including the concept of rights, could be deployed in the fight against colonial domination, as in the case of the Haitian Revolution. It cannot be claimed that Mary Wollstonecraft is the global originator of a universal feminism, but the critical tools she offered have a bearing on enduring problems with global scope.

The most striking convergences occur, of course, in the area of women's rights. The feeling that she is a fellow traveller has, if anything, grown since the start of the millennium (Figure 8).

8. Stencil of Mary Wollstonecraft by Stewy; street art on the wall of
Newington Green Unitarian Chapel, created 12 March 2013 in support
of the campaign 'Mary on the Green'. It recalls Virginia Woolf's
description of Wollstonecraft as 'alive and active ... we hear her voice
and trace her influence even now among the living'.

Many terms in the evolving lexicon of feminist analysis resonate with problems identified by Wollstonecraft. The concept of 'gender apartheid', for instance, seems to coincide with her condemnation in *Rights of Woman* of those 'tyrants of every denomination, from the weak king to the weak father of a family' who '*force* all women, by denying them civil and political rights, to remain immured in their families groping in the dark'. Or take 'coercive control', a recently defined category of domestic abuse that involves psychological and emotional persecution short of physical assault, and has now entered the statute book in several countries. It does not affect women exclusively, but the majority of victims are female. Wollstonecraft attempted to represent the evil of this form of abuse in *Wrongs of Woman*, and was met with incomprehension. Now that it has been named, her purpose springs into focus. It is dispiriting that structures of oppression can barely alter over centuries, but the very act of identifying continuities may be a warrant to share her optimism.

Perhaps the greatest change, another altered 'stream in popular opinion', is the new openness around mental illness. This has cleared the way for reassessment of aspects of Mary Wollstonecraft's life and life writing touching on childhood trauma, depression, and attempted suicide. These aspects of her story have often been used to discredit her. Even serious biographers have dismissed her expressions of frustration or confusion, mockingly, as 'moaning' or 'hysteria'. Very few of her letters were published before 1979, and these are only a small fraction of the many she wrote that have been lost, but they show her efforts to develop a feminist language of interiority, vulnerable, complex, resistant to stereotype, at once despairing and resilient.

Wollstonecraft today is a towering figure in the history of the Anglo-American campaign for women's rights. The memorial sculpture 'For Mary Wollstonecraft' at Newington Green, unveiled in 2020 after years of fundraising by the 'Mary on the Green' campaign, represents her spirit as that of an emancipated everywoman. Remarkable archival work has been undertaken, most notably by Eileen Hunt, to show the extraordinary reach of her reputation and her ideas, from the 1790s continuously through the 19th century to the present day, spanning Europe, the United States, and the colonial cultures of the West Indies, South America, and India. At the same time, similar archival excavation of other traditions of feminist thought and activism puts in question her historical primacy. The best-known works by Wollstonecraft were translated throughout continental Europe and the facts of her biography were a matter of record, but there are other candidates for the role of catalyst even there. That is of course a given in other parts of the world, the Middle East, most of Asia, and Africa, where she was almost entirely unknown and untranslated. Her influence, if it has come at all, will have dated from the 1970s or later, and therefore post-dates the impact of other pioneering campaigners.

What is notable, when surveying the development of women's movements across the globe, is the recurrence of a charismatic figure who, like Mary Wollstonecraft, speaks her freedom into existence while being willing, openly, to break with social norms. Wollstonecraft presents a relatively well-documented case of a woman dedicated to *living* the principles of feminism, regardless of custom and the risk of disgrace and prosecution, while publicizing arguments for equal rights. There is much to be gained from seeing her achievements anew, informed by what one might call the field of comparative global feminisms.

Timeline of Wollstonecraft's life and works

1759	Born on 27 April in Spitalfields, London.
1763–8	The Wollstonecraft family moves successively to Epping and to Barking, on the outskirts of London, then to Beverley in Yorkshire, where they remain for six years.
1774	The Wollstonecraft family moves to Hoxton, a suburb north of London, where MW is mentored by the Reverend Mr Clare and his wife, and befriends Frances Blood.
1776	The Wollstonecraft family moves to Laugherne, Wales.
1777	The Wollstonecraft family moves to Walworth, a suburb south of London.
1778	MW works as a paid companion to Mrs Dawson of Bath, and accompanies her on visits to Southampton and Windsor.
1781	Mrs Wollstonecraft becomes terminally ill and MW returns to the family home to nurse her.
1782	Following the death of Mrs Wollstonecraft, MW's father remarries and moves to Wales. MW moves in with the family of Frances Blood and helps to support them. Her sister Eliza marries Meredith Bishop (Oct.).
1783	Eliza gives birth to a daughter in August and suffers from mental illness. When MW provides support, Eliza indicates that she has suffered marital abuse.

1784	MW assists Eliza in escaping from her husband, but they are forced to leave the child behind and she dies within the year. They join with the third Wollstonecraft sister, Everina, and Fanny Blood to establish a school, first briefly in Islington, then at Newington Green, north of London.
1785	Frances Blood departs to marry the Irish merchant Hugh Skeys in Lisbon. When she becomes pregnant MW travels to assist, but Fanny dies soon after giving birth in late November. MW returns to Newington Green (Dec.).
1786	Financial problems lead to closure of the school, MW finds employment as a governess in the family of Viscount Kingsborough in Mitchelstown (Co. Cork), Ireland, and her sisters enter positions as teachers.
1787	*Thoughts on the Education of Daughters* published by Joseph Johnson. MW stays in Dublin and Bristol with the Kingsboroughs. MW is dismissed from the post of governess (Aug.), visits Joseph Johnson with the manuscript of a novel, and is offered employment as a staff writer (Sept.).
1788	*Mary, A Fiction, Original Stories from Real Life*, and *Of the Importance of Religious Opinions* (trans. from Necker), published by JJ. MW starts reviewing for the monthly journal *The Analytical Review*.
1789	*The Female Reader* published by JJ under the pseudonym of Mr Cresswick.
1790	*Young Grandison* (adaptation of trans. from Margareta Geertruid de Cambon-van der Werken), *Elements of Morality* (trans. from Christian Gotthilf Salzmann), and (Nov.) *A Vindication of the Rights of Men* published by JJ. A second edition of *Rights of Men* published (Dec.) with MW's name on the title page.
1791	Second edition of *Original Stories from Real Life* published with original illustrations by William Blake.
1792	*A Vindication of the Rights of Woman* published by JJ (Jan.); a second edition appears in Dec. MW travels to Paris (Dec.) for a short visit.

1793	Following the execution of Louis XVI, on 1 February France declares war on Britain and MW decides to remain in Paris. She moves to Neuilly outside the city and begins a relationship with the American entrepreneur and writer Gilbert Imlay. In September she returns to Paris and is registered as Imlay's wife at the American Embassy.
1794	MW moves to Le Havre (Jan.) to live with Imlay during the final stages of pregnancy. On 14 May, her daughter Frances Imlay is born. *An Historical and Moral View of the Origin and Progress of the French Revolution* published by JJ (Dec.).
1795	MW joins Imlay in London (Apr.). She discovers his infidelity and attempts suicide (May). From June to September she travels through Scandinavia and Germany with infant Fanny and her maid Marguerite Fournée as a legal envoy for Imlay to investigate a business fraud. On return, she again attempts suicide (Oct.) and breaks with Imlay.
1796	*Letters Written During a Short Residence in Sweden, Norway and Denmark* published by JJ (Jan.). MW begins a relationship with William Godwin (Aug.).
1797	MW, four months pregnant, marries Godwin in St Pancras Old Church on 29 March. Her second daughter, Mary Godwin, is born on 30 August and MW dies of septicaemia on 10 September.
1798	*Memoirs of the Author of A Vindication of the Rights of Woman* by Godwin is published by JJ (Jan.). *Posthumous Works*, mainly composed of manuscript writings edited by Godwin, including *The Wrongs of Woman: or, Maria. A Fragment*, 'The Cave of Fancy', letters to Imlay and to Joseph Johnson, an essay on poetry, and an educational sketch, appear at the same time.

Further reading

Primary

The Collected Letters of Mary Wollstonecraft, ed. Janet Todd (Columbia University Press, 2003).

Letters Written during a Short Residence in Sweden, Norway and Denmark, ed. Tone Brekke and Jon Mee (Oxford World's Classics, 2009).

'Mary, A Fiction' and 'The Wrongs of Woman, or Maria', ed. Gary Kelly (Oxford World's Classics, 2007).

'A Vindication of the Rights of Men' and 'A Vindication of the Rights of Woman', ed. Sylvana Tomaselli (Cambridge University Press, 1995).

A Vindication of the Rights of Woman, ed. Deidre Shauna Lynch (rev. edn Norton, 2009).

The Works of Mary Wollstonecraft, ed. Janet Todd and Marilyn Butler, 7 volumes (William Pickering, 1989).

Biographies

Caroline Franklin, *Mary Wollstonecraft: A Literary Life* (Palgrave Macmillan, 2004).

William Godwin, *Memoirs of the Author of A Vindication of the Rights of Woman*, ed. Pamela Clemit and Gina Luria Walker (Broadview, 2001).

Lyndall Gordon, *Vindication: A Life of Mary Wollstonecraft* (Little, Brown, 2005).

Daisy Hay, *Dinner with Joseph Johnson: Books and Friendship in a Revolutionary Age* (Chatto & Windus, 2022).

Jane Moore, *Mary Wollstonecraft*, Writers and Their Work series (Liverpool University Press, 1999).

Janet Todd, *Mary Wollstonecraft: A Revolutionary Life* (Phoenix Press, 2000).

Claire Tomalin, *The Life and Death of Mary Wollstonecraft* (rev. edn Penguin, 1992).

Wil Verhoeven, *Gilbert Imlay: Citizen of the World* (Pickering & Chatto, 2008).

Key essay collections

Sandrine Bergès, Eileen Hunt Botting, and Alan Coffee, eds, *The Wollstonecraftian Mind* (Routledge, 2020).

Sandrine Bergès and Alan Coffee, eds, *The Social and Political Philosophy of Mary Wollstonecraft* (Oxford University Press, 2016).

Sonia Hofkosh, ed., *Mary Wollstonecraft, Even Now* (Romantic Circles Praxis Series, 2019) (web open access).

Claudia Johnson, ed., *The Cambridge Companion to Mary Wollstonecraft* (Cambridge University Press, 2002).

Nancy E. Johnson and Paul Keen, eds, *Mary Wollstonecraft in Context* (Cambridge University Press, 2020).

Enit Karafili Steiner, ed., *Called to Civil Existence: Mary Wollstonecraft's Influence on the Women Writers of Her Day* (Rodopi, 2014).

Chapter 1: First of a new genus

Mary Hays, 'Memoirs of Mary Wollstonecraft', from *Annual Necrology for 1797-8* (1800), extract in Godwin, *Memoirs* (Broadview, 2001), pp. 188–90.

Virginia Woolf, 'Mary Wollstonecraft', in *The Common Reader: Volume 2* (Penguin, 2019).

Chapter 2: The making of a feminist

Saba Bahar, *Mary Wollstonecraft's Social and Aesthetic Philosophy: An Eve to Please Me* (Palgrave Macmillan, 2002).

E. J. Clery, 'Mary Wollstonecraft: A Feminist Exile in Paris', *Litteraria Pragensia: Studies in Literature and Culture*, 29.57 (July 2019), pp. 29–46 (web open access).

Suzanne Desan, *The Family on Trial in Revolutionary Paris* (University of California Press, 2004).

Gary Kelly, *Revolutionary Feminism: The Mind and Career of Mary Wollstonecraft* (Macmillan, 1996).

Ashley Taubert, *Mary Wollstonecraft and the Accent of the Feminine* (Palgrave Macmillan, 2002).

Sylvana Tomaselli, 'The Most Public Sphere of All: The Family', in Elizabeth Eger, Charlotte Grant, Cliona O Gallchoir, and Penny Warburton, eds, *Women, Writing and the Public Sphere, 1700–1830* (Cambridge University Press, 2001), pp. 239–56.

Margaret Walters, *Feminism: A Very Short Introduction* (Oxford University Press, 2005).

Chapter 3: Educator

Laura Kirkley, 'Elements of the Other: Mary Wollstonecraft and Translation', in Gillian Dow, ed., *Translators, Interpreters, Mediators: Women Writers 1700–1900* (Peter Lang, 2007), pp. 83–98.

Laura Kirkley, *Mary Wollstonecraft: Cosmopolitan* (Edinburgh University Press, 2022).

Mitzi Myers, 'Impeccable Governesses, Rational Dames, and Moral Mothers: Mary Wollstonecraft and the Female Tradition in Georgian Children's Books', *Children's Literature*, 14 (1986), pp. 31–59.

Alan Richardson, 'Mary Wollstonecraft on Education', in Johnson, ed., *Cambridge Companion to Mary Wollstonecraft*, pp. 24–42.

Chapter 4: Political thinker

Isabelle Bour, 'Mary Wollstonecraft as Historian in *An Historical and Moral View of the Origin and Progress of the French Revolution; and the Effect it has Produced in Europe* (1794)', *Études Épistémè*, 17 (2010) (web open access).

Moira Ferguson, 'Mary Wollstonecraft and the Problematic of Slavery', *Feminist Review*, 42 (Autumn 1992), pp. 82–102.

Lena Halldenius, *Mary Wollstonecraft and Feminist Republicanism: Independence, Rights and the Experience of Unfreedom* (Routledge, 2016).

Daniel O'Neill, *The Burke–Wollstonecraft Debate: Savagery, Civilization, and Democracy* (The Pennsylvania State University Press, 2007).

Catherine Packham, '"The Common Grievance of the Revolution": Bread, the Grain Trade, and Political Economy in Mary Wollstonecraft's *View of the French Revolution*', *European Romantic Review*, 25.6 (2014), pp. 705–22.

Jane Rendall, '"The Grand Causes which Combine to Carry Mankind Forward": Wollstonecraft, History and Revolution', *Women's Writing*, 4.2 (1997), pp. 155–72.

Virginia Sapiro, *A Vindication of Political Virtue: The Political Theory of Mary Wollstonecraft* (University of Chicago Press, 1992).

Chapter 5: Romantic

Claudia Johnson, *Equivocal Beings: Politics, Gender, and Sentimentality in the 1790s: Wollstonecraft, Radcliffe, Burney, Austen* (University of Chicago Press, 1995).

Mitzi Myers, 'Unfinished Business: Wollstonecraft's *Maria*', *The Wordsworth Circle*, 11.2 (Spring 1980), pp. 107–14.

Martina Reuter, 'Jean-Jacques Rousseau and Mary Wollstonecraft on the Imagination', *British Journal for the History of Philosophy*, 25.6 (2017), pp. 1138–60.

Anka Ryall and Catherine Sandback-Dahlström, eds, *Mary Wollstonecraft's Journey to Scandanavia: Essays*, Stockholm Studies in English XCIX (Almqvist & Wiksell International, 2003).

Barbara Taylor, *Mary Wollstonecraft and the Feminist Imagination* (Cambridge University Press, 2003).

John Whale, *Imagination under Pressure, 1789–1832: Aesthetics, Politics and Utility* (Cambridge University Press, 2000).

Susan J. Wolfson, *Romantic Interactions: Social Being and the Turns of Literary Action* (The Johns Hopkins University Press, 2010).

Susan J. Wolfson, *On Mary Wollstonecraft's 'A Vindication of the Rights of Woman'* (Columbia, 2023).

Chapter 6: Reintroducing Mary Wollstonecraft

Brenda Ayres, *Betwixt and Between: The Biographies of Mary Wollstonecraft* (Anthem, 2017).

Eileen Hunt Botting, 'Wollstonecraft in Europe, 1792–1904: A Revisionist Reception History', *History of European Ideas*, 39.4 (2013), pp. 503–27.

Eileen Hunt Botting, *Portraits of Wollstonecraft*, 2 volumes
(Bloomsbury, 2021). Volume I: *Portraiture, Reception and
Biographies, 1785–1913*. Volume II: *Literary Depictions and Global
Feminisms, 1801–2020*.

Barbara Caine, 'Victorian Feminism and the Ghost of Mary
Wollstonecraft', *Women's Writing*, 4.2 (1997), pp. 261–75.

Harriet Devine Jump, ed., *Mary Wollstonecraft and the Critics,
1788–2001*, 2 volumes (Routledge, 2003).

Cora Kaplan, 'Mary Wollstonecraft's Reception and Legacies', in
Johnson, ed., *Cambridge Companion to Mary Wollstonecraft*,
pp. 246–69.

Jane Moore, ed., *Mary Wollstonecraft* (Routledge, 2012).

Julie Murray, 'Mary Wollstonecraft, Feminist Killjoy', in Hofkosh, ed.,
Mary Wollstonecraft, Even Now (2019) (web open access).

Index

For the benefit of digital users, indexed terms that span two pages (e.g., 52–53) may, on occasion, appear on only one of those pages.

Index

EIGHTEENTH CENTURY BRITAIN

A Very Short Introduction

Paul Langford

Eighteenth-century Britain is sometimes thought of as sedate, oligarchical, and conservative.

Paul Langford's *Very Short Introduction* to eighteenth-century Britain reveals its essential vitality as Britain evolved into a great power, an industrial giant, and a dynamic commercial society. The transforming effect of a hundred years is concisely narrated in its diversity and complexity.

www.oup.com/vsi

ROMANTICISM
A Very Short Introduction
Michael Ferber

What is Romanticism? In this *Very Short Introduction*
Michael Ferber answers this by considering who the romantics
were and looks at what they had in common – their ideas, beliefs,
commitments, and tastes. He looks at the birth and growth
of Romanticism throughout Europe and the Americas, and
examines various types of Romantic literature, music, painting,
religion, and philosophy. Focusing on topics, Ferber looks at the
rising prestige of the poet; Romanticism as a religious trend;
Romantic philosophy and science; Romantic responses to the
French Revolution; and the condition of women. Using examples
and quotations he presents a clear insight into this very diverse
movement.

www.oup.com/vsi

THE BODY
A Very Short Introduction
Chris Shilling

The human body is thought of conventionally as a biological entity, with its longevity, morbidity, size and even appearance determined by genetic factors immune to the influence of society or culture. Since the mid-1980s, however, there has been a rising awareness of how our bodies, and our perception of them, are influenced by the social, cultural and material contexts in which humans live.

Drawing on studies of sex and gender, education, governance, the economy, and religion, Chris Shilling demonstrates how our physical being allows us to affect the material and virtual world around us, yet also enables governments to shape and direct our thoughts and actions. Revealing how social relationships, cultural images, and technological and medical advances shape our perceptions and awareness, he exposes the limitations of traditional Western traditions of thought that elevate the mind over the body as that which defines us as human. Dealing with issues ranging from cosmetic and transplant surgery, the performance of gendered identities, the commodification of bodies and body parts, and the violent consequences of competing conceptions of the body as sacred, Shilling provides a compelling account of why body matters present contemporary societies with a series of urgent and inescapable challenges.

www.oup.com/vsi

FREE SPEECH
A Very Short Introduction
Nigel Warburton

'I disapprove of what you say, but I will defend to the death your right to say it' This slogan, attributed to Voltaire, is frequently quoted by defenders of free speech. Yet it is rare to find anyone prepared to defend all expression in every circumstance, especially if the views expressed incite violence. So where do the limits lie? What is the real value of free speech? Here, Nigel Warburton offers a concise guide to important questions facing modern society about the value and limits of free speech: Where should a civilized society draw the line? Should we be free to offend other people's religion? Are there good grounds for censoring pornography? Has the Internet changed everything? This Very Short Introduction is a thought-provoking, accessible, and up-to-date examination of the liberal assumption that free speech is worth preserving at any cost.

> 'The genius of Nigel Warburton's *Free Speech* lies not only in its extraordinary clarity and incisiveness. Just as important is the way Warburton addresses freedom of speech - and attempts to stifle it - as an issue for the 21st century. More than ever, we need this book.'

> **Denis Dutton, University of Canterbury, New Zealand**

LEADERSHIP
A Very Short Introduction
Keith Grint

In this *Very Short Introduction* Keith Grint prompts the reader to rethink their understanding of what leadership is. He examines the way leadership has evolved from its earliest manifestations in ancient societies, highlighting the beginnings of leadership writings through Plato, Sun Tzu, Machiavelli and others, to consider the role of the social, economic, and political context undermining particular modes of leadership. Exploring the idea that leaders cannot exist without followers, and recognising that we all have diverse experiences and assumptions of leadership, Grint looks at the practice of management, its history, future, and influence on all aspects of society.